6.99

1.815
Nie

D1128481

1-02

THE
Bread
COOKBOOK

THE
Bread
COOKBOOK

Ann Nicol

SMITHMARK

A SALAMANDER BOOK

Published by Salamander Books Ltd
129-137 York Way
London N7 9LG
United Kingdom

This edition published in 1995 by
SMITHMARK Publishers,
a division of U.S. Media Holdings, Inc.,
16 East 32nd Street,
New York, NY 10016.

1 3 5 7 9 8 6 4 2

ISBN 0–8317–1001–2

SMITHMARK books are available for bulk
purchase for sales promotion and premium use.
For details, write or call the manager of Special Sales,
SMITHMARK Publishers,
16 East 32nd Street, New York
NY 10016; (212) 532 – 6600.

All correspondence concerning the content of this volume should be addressed to
Salamander Books Ltd.

CREDITS
COMMISSIONING EDITOR: *Anne McDowall*
EDITOR: *Veronica Sperling*
AMERICAN EDITOR: *Barbara Butler*
DESIGNER: *Carole Perks*
PHOTOGRAPHER: *Sue Jorgensen*
HOME ECONOMIST: *Ann Nicol*
STYLIST: *Maria Kelly*
INDEXER: *Hilary Bird*
COLOR SEPARATION: *P & W Graphics*

Printed in Singapore

ACKNOWLEDGEMENTS
The author and publishers would like to thank David Mellor Ltd., Sloane Street,
London and Kenwood Ltd. for loaning equipment for photography.

Contents

Author's Introduction 6

Introduction 8

Country Breads 18

Enriched Breads 30

Continental Breads 42

Breads from the British Isles 54

American Breads 62

Eastern Breads 68

Festive Breads 72

Breads with Fillings 84

Breads without Yeast 90

Index 96

Author's Introduction

Making and baking bread really is one of life's simple pleasures. If you have never experienced the luxury of home-baked bread before, then now is the time to start baking. You won't need expensive ingredients or equipment, but you will need to put aside a little extra time and lots of enthusiasm, for what I hope will become a life-long passion.

Why should you make the effort? Because the smell of home-baked bread is delightful, it's good to eat, doesn't contain colorings, chemicals or additives and it tastes simply delicious. There really is nothing quite like it.

It's good for you, body and soul. The joy of making a dough that really rises gives you a tremendous feeling of creativity and satisfaction. Knead your stress, worries and bad temper away into a piece of dough, and you'll come out of the kitchen feeling much better for it.

I adore baking and bakeries, and on my travels I always seek out the local bakery to look for regional specialities and find out what other bakers are creating. I started home baking when I was a penniless student, and found that not only was home-baked bread economical, but also I got hooked on working with doughs and baking them.

Breadmaking is not difficult, there is no great mystery but simple rules do need to be followed. Unlike cake or pastry baking, you can't really spoil a dough – in fact the heavier handed you are the better! The great thing about breadmaking is it really is difficult to fail! The one main rule to bear in mind is that too much heat will kill off yeast. So as long as you avoid using hot liquids or standing the dough in too hot a place, you can't go wrong. If a dough doesn't rise, don't worry, just leave it for a little longer. If you overcook a loaf, you'll get a really crispy crust.

Ingredients like stonemilled and unbleached flours may be more difficult to find but are well worth looking for, as is fresh whole yeast, which gives the very best texture to all breads. Remember your bread will only be as good as the ingredients that go into it, so seek out the best quality you can find.

Although perceived as time consuming, breadmaking really can be fitted into the course of your day, with a little planning. Or if you have a really hectic working schedule, wind down and indulge in some therapeutic weekend baking.

Once you've made and worked with a simple dough, seen it rise and baked it, I'm sure you'll want to continue and try more varied recipes. This book starts with simple white and wholewheat breads, then goes on to tackle enriched doughs and international breads, many of which are baked for festivals and special occasions. I hope you'll try all of these and share with me the wonderful pleasure of making your own home-baked breads.

Ann Nicol

Introduction

Learning about all the many flours and ingredients used for breadmaking is fascinating, and these are described in the following pages. To help you understand the basic techniques involved, these have been described in detail, with plenty of hints and tips and photographs. These are followed by an easy step-by-step recipe for making traditional white bread. There are a wide variety of finishes and toppings for bread and these are shown on pages 16-17, along with ideas for shaping bread, to help you add your own individual touch to the bread you bake.

Ingredients

Breadmaking is an age old craft. From way back the Ancient Greeks worshipped the goddess of cereals, Dementer, and there are numerous references in the Bible to breadmaking. Through the ages the same basic grains and yeasts have always been used.

Flours

Wheat flour is the most commonly milled flour to be used for breadmaking. Sometimes other grains are used, either alone or mixed into wheat flour, giving a particular flavor and texture to a bread.

White flour The bran and wheatgerm are removed from white flours during the milling process. As nutrients are lost this way, the law requires that iron and B vitamins be added to white flours.

Bread flour is made from hard wheats which have a high proportion of protein. This means that dough can develop and stretch to contain more air.

All-purpose flour contains blends of wheat lower in protein content than bread flour, but which contains enough protein to make good yeast bread in the home, yet not too much for good quick breads.

Wholewheat flour contains 100 percent extraction of the wheat grain. All the bran and wheatgerm is present and this flour gives a moist, close texture to breads.

Brown or wheatmeal flours contain 85 percent of the wheat kernel and most of the wheatgerm, but a little of the bran has been removed to give a lighter texture.

Granary or mixed grain flour is usually of 85 percent extraction and contains malted wheat and rye grains,

BELOW, LEFT TO RIGHT: Bread flour, wholewheat flour, wheatmeal flour, cornmeal, buckwheat flour.

which give a delicious texture and flavor to bread.

Cornmeal is a bright yellow, gritty flour milled from corn kernels. It comes in a fine and a coarse texture. It lacks protein so must be mixed with wheat flours for yeast baking, or with rising agents like baking powder or baking soda for quick breads.

Oats lack gluten proteins, but can be mixed into wheatflours for delicious moist-textured breads. Oats take up moisture, so soak them before use or add extra liquid to a dough containing oats.

Rye flour contains gum-like substances that can inhibit the rising of bread, so it is usually mixed with wheat flour for a lighter, springy texture. Rye flour produces a characteristically dark, delicious chewy bread.

Buckwheat flour is a dark grey, fine-textured, low-gluten flour. Use it for pancakes or mix with other flours.

Stoneground flours have a coarser texture but a fuller flavor. As they have been milled between two stones, not steel rollers, these flours are more expensive, but they do produce delicious results with a mellow flavor.

Unbleached flours have a natural creamy color and are left longer to age naturally. As they have not been bleached or treated with chemicals they have a completely natural composition and produce beautiful white breads with a fuller flavor. They are more expensive, but are worth the extra money.

Storing Flour

Keep flour in its bag in a cool, dry place. (Damp flour weighs more, so will affect the recipe.) If your kitchen is damp or steamy, use a storage jar, but remember to use all the flour before refilling – don't add new flour to old.

Plain white flour will keep for 6 months. Brown or wholewheat flours will only keep for 3 months and because of their higher fat content can become rancid.

Salt

Salt is an essential ingredient in breadmaking, and not just a flavoring. Salt controls the rising action of the yeast by preventing it from fermenting too quickly. It strengthens the gluten and adds flavor. The proportions are 1-2 tsp. per 1 lb of flour. Adding too much salt slows down the action of the yeast, so follow the exact amount stated in the recipe.

Yeasts

Yeast is a living organism, which feeds on carbohydrates, or the starches and sugars present in flour. It will start to grow when it comes into contact with moisture, warmth and starchy substances. As it converts the starch into sugar, this sets free carbonic acid gas, which spreads through the dough making it light, porous and spongy.

BELOW, LEFT TO RIGHT: Oats, rye flour, stoneground flour, granary flour, unbleached flour.

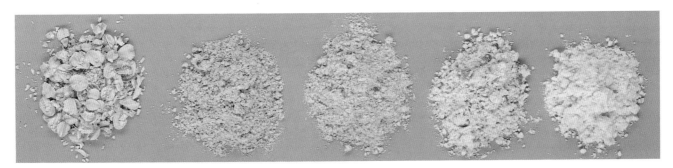

Fresh yeast should be creamy beige, solid and compressed in one piece, and fresh smelling. If it has crumbled or is grey in color it is not so fresh and will not work as well. Once a block of yeast is broken up it starts to dry out and lose its potency. Store fresh yeast in the coldest part of the refrigerator in a lidded plastic box with a few ventilation holes in it or loosely wrapped in plastic wrap. It should keep well for up to four weeks.

Fresh yeast gives breads a superior flavor and a really springy texture. Fresh yeast is sold in 0.6 oz cakes in grocery stores. Each cake is equivalent to 1 package of dry yeast, which contains 2¼ teaspoons. Wrap unused yeast in plastic wrap and freeze quickly. It will keep for up to six weeks in the freezer and this is a good way of ensuring you have a supply handy.

Dry yeast is useful to have in the pantry, and is sold in most supermarkets. It needs to be added to liquid and left to reconstitute for about 15 to 20 minutes before adding to flour. It is highly concentrated and you will need just half the amount of the weight of fresh yeast. Weigh or measure dry yeast very carefully; don't be tempted to use more than half the weight of fresh, as the bread will go stale and dry quickly.

Dry yeast comes in foil packages or small jars in the form of small beige granules. Each package of dry yeast contains 2¼ teaspoons. Once opened, keep the container airtight as the larger the airspace in the container, the less well the yeast will keep. The packages, however, keep the yeast really airtight and supply you with just the right amount every time.

Quick-rise yeast This yeast comes in a powder form in packages and is widely available from most supermarkets. It is made from a very strong strain of yeast which does not need reconstituting with water before use. The yeast is mixed directly into the flour, then liquid is added to make a dough. Breads made from this yeast usually need only one rising.

Storage and freezing tips

Most breads are best eaten about two hours after baking. Don't be tempted to eat bread fresh from the oven as it has an indigestible doughy texture, but will harden on cooling.

Although it is preferable to eat bread on the day of baking, most will store well for two days in a bread box or crock or cool pantry.

Bread freezes very well, so it is worth making a double batch – one for eating and one for the freezer. After baking and cooling, freeze in foil or in an airtight plastic bag. For best results, thaw at room temperature, not in the microwave. Some breads, such as the Italian ones, are delicious if gently warmed through after freezing.

Liquids and Fats

The liquid used to make bread can be either water, milk or a mixture of both. Sometimes cream or yogurt are added to produce a bread with a moist texture and with better keeping qualities.

Liquids must be no hotter than 100°F, a temperature that can be obtained by using one-third boiling water to two-thirds cold water. A liquid that is too hot will kill off the yeast and the dough will not rise.

The best way to use any liquid is at blood heat. To test for blood heat, dab a few drops of liquid on your wrist at the pulse point. If the liquid feels warm, it is too hot. You should not be able to feel any heat at all in the liquid, neither should it feel cold.

Fats are added to doughs to enrich them and to give softness and color. They also delay staling.

Softened or melted butter or vegetable margarine can be easily rubbed or kneaded into doughs. Vegetable oils, and olive or nut oils can also be used for flavor.

Equipment

You won't need much special equipment for breadmaking, and most of the following items can be found in the average kitchen.

Accurate kitchen scales These are a must for measuring. Battery operated digital scales are very good for weighing small amounts of yeast.

A graduated measuring cup This is essential for measuring the correct amounts of liquid.

Measuring spoons Always use a set of proper graduated measures, not cutlery, for best results, particularly when measuring dried yeast and salt.

A large deep mixing bowl The deeper the bowl the better, for mixing doughs and leaving them to rise.

Baking sheets and pans Thick, heavy duty baking sheets are good for yeast baking as the thinner ones tend to buckle on heating and can spoil the shapes of doughs.

Old-fashioned loaf pans well used and blackened with age, are wonderful for baking. Look for these at tag sales and charity shops. If you are buying new ones, thick-based non-stick pans are good. Remember the more you pay for bakeware, the better durability and service it will give you.

Grease pans well with unsalted butter or vegetable fat before use. If using oven-proof glass baking pans, decrease the oven temperature 25°F.

Plastic wrap and large size plastic bags Both are useful for covering and enclosing doughs during rising. Coat lightly with oil before using.

Table top mixer A dough hook attachment on a table top mixer will help take the hard work out of kneading. Don't be tempted to knead in a food processor, as the blades will tear the dough.

Water spray Salt water sprayed through a fine garden or plant spray directly onto breads in the oven helps create steam and so achieve a crisp crust. A shallow meat roasting pan, filled with water and placed in the oven, has a similar effect.

BELOW: *Most breadmaking equipment can be found in the average kitchen; a selection of different pans is useful.*

Basic Techniques for Making Bread

Making a yeast liquid

This is usually the first step in a bread recipe.

Fresh yeast should be sprinkled into lukewarm liquid and gently stirred in. Don't overmix or cream the yeast with the sugar as this gives an unpleasant yeasty flavor.

Dry yeast granules must be reconstituted before use. Stir the yeast into the lukewarm liquid with a pinch of granulated sugar and leave for 10 to 20 minutes until the liquid is dissolved and frothy. If the mixture does not froth, it means the yeast is stale, so don't use it.

Quick-rise yeast is a new strong strain of powdered yeast sold in 7 g foil envelopes. It must not be reactivated in liquid, but is added directly to the dry ingredients. It normally needs only one rising.

Making a batter

Recipes which are enriched with eggs or fats, start with a sponge batter. Rich ingredients slow down the rising of dough, so a small amount of flour is whisked into the yeast liquid, and left to froth for about 20 minutes. This

BELOW, LEFT TO RIGHT: Sprinkling fresh yeast into water; adding quick-rise yeast to dry ingredients; making a batter.

is then added to the other ingredients to help give an extra boost to the rising process.

Mixing

Once the yeast liquid is added to the flour, a soft dough is formed and this must be kneaded well to stretch and expand a protein in the flour called gluten. This gives a soft stretchy dough that will allow air bubbles to form and give a light bread.

Kneading

Turn the dough on to a lightly floured surface, fold it in half towards you then push down and away from you. Give the dough a quarter turn and repeat folding and pushing in a rocking action, using the heel of your hand. The dough will be soft and sticky at first, but it will become more elastic as you knead it, so don't be tempted to add more flour. Don't pull or tear at the dough or you will break the strands of gluten that you are working hard to develop. Knead with a gently rocking motion for about 5 to 10 minutes until the dough feels soft, smooth and silky and elastic. You can knead in a table top mixer with a dough hook attachment but it is still best to finish off the kneading by hand, to get the correct feel of the dough.

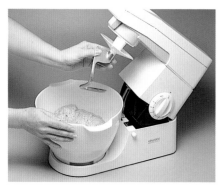

Rising

After the dough is made, it must be left for a period of time to allow the yeast to do its work and aerate the dough. Place the dough back in its mixing bowl and cover with lightly oiled plastic wrap. Slowly risen dough makes the best bread, so leave the dough at room temperature or in a very gently heated place (too high a temperature will kill off the yeast). Most doughs will take 1½ to 2 hours to rise. Doughs can be risen overnight in a refrigerator, but halve the quantity of yeast.

Knocking back

A risen dough will have large bubbles of gas distributed through it. Turn the risen dough out onto an unfloured surface, punch down all over to flatten out the air, then knead again until smooth and elastic. Don't use any extra flour as it will spoil the final texture of the baked bread.

ABOVE, LEFT TO RIGHT: Using the dough hook on a table-top mixer; punching down the risen dough; covering the dough with lightly oiled plastic wrap to rise.

Proving and baking

The dough is now shaped, covered with oiled plastic wrap again, and left to double in size (unless using quick-rise yeast, see page 10). A very hot temperature is needed to destroy the yeast and stop it working. Use the hottest part of your oven and set it at 400°F to 450°F, depending on the recipe. When the bread is baked, turn it out of the pan and tap it underneath with your knuckles – it should sound hollow. Turn the loaves out of the pans and bake upside down on the oven shelf for 5 minutes to crisp the crust all over.

BELOW, LEFT TO RIGHT: Braiding dough; shaping a cottage loaf; sprinkling poppy seeds on shaped rolls (see page 16).

Traditional White Bread

Use this recipe to batch bake a selection of loaves and rolls (see page 16 for ideas for shaping bread). If this is more than you need, you'll find fresh bread freezes very well.

Yeast Liquid
2 packages DRY YEAST
2 tsp. GRANULATED SUGAR
3 cups LUKEWARM WATER
or
2 cakes FRESH YEAST
3 cups LUKEWARM WATER

Other Ingredients
$10\frac{1}{2}$ cups BREAD FLOUR
4 tsp. SALT
1 tbsp. GRANULATED SUGAR
$\frac{1}{4}$ cup LARD OR WHITE VEGETABLE SHORTENING

Mix the flour and salt, add the sugar and rub in the fat. Add the yeast liquid and mix to a soft dough.

Turn out and knead for 10 minutes until smooth, elastic and no longer sticky. Use the heel of your hand to stretch and turn the dough.

Stir the dry yeast and sugar into the water and leave until frothy – about 10 minutes. If using fresh yeast, blend with the water.

Cover with lightly oiled plastic wrap and leave in a warm place until the dough is puffy and has doubled in size, this takes about 1¼ hours. Turn out and knead for 5 minutes to knock out all the air.

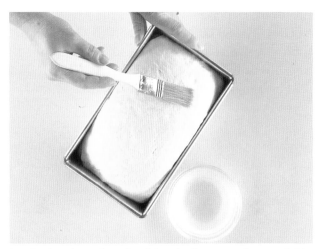

Brush the risen dough with salted water, then sprinkle over flour before baking. This gives a crispy crust.

Divide into 3 equal pieces and shape into loaves or rolls. Place in greased 8½ × 4¼ × 2¾-inch loaf pans or place rolls on oiled baking sheets. Cover with oiled plastic wrap and leave to prove until doubled in size.

Preheat the oven to 450°F. Bake loaves for 30 to 40 minutes, rolls for 15 to 20 minutes, until bread sounds hollow when tapped. For a crusty finish, remove from the pans and bake 5 minutes longer.

MAKES 3 × 1 LB LOAVES

Finishes and Toppings

Part of the fun of making bread is the wide variety of different shapes, textures and toppings you can use. Experiment using any type of dough, and discover the way that seeds, flour or a crusty finish will transform a plain bread into your own unique creation.

Finishes

Shiny finish Glaze the dough with a beaten egg white or egg yolk, or whole egg beaten with a pinch of salt, before baking.

Crisp crust Brush the dough with salted water, or spray with salted water during baking.

Soft finish Brush the dough with light cream, then dust with flour half way through the baking. Cover rolls or bread with a clean dry cloth when baked, and leave covered until completely cool.

Toppings

Glaze bread after shaping and proving the dough, and sprinkle over any of the following: poppy seeds, oats, barley, sesame seeds, caraway seeds, rye or wheat flakes, cornmeal, or semolina; or dust the dough with plain white or wholewheat flour.

Variations

Try these shape variations, using any of the basic doughs:

Cottage loaf

Use one third quantiy risen dough. Roll two thirds into a large ball and place on a greased baking sheet. Roll the remaining third into a smaller ball and place on top.

Flour a wooden spoon handle and make a hole through the center of both balls. Cover and leave to double in size, brush with salt glaze and bake at 450°F for 35 minutes.

Vienna bread

Shape half the quantity of risen dough into two flat sausages. Place on greased baking sheets and brush with beaten egg. Sprinkle liberally with poppy seeds and leave to prove until doubled in size. Slash down the center with a razor blade and bake as above.

Bloomer

Shape half the quantity of risen white bread dough into a fat sausage. Brush with beaten egg and and make slanting cuts across the top before baking as above.

Morning rolls

Shape a half quantity of risen dough into 12 flat rounds and brush tops with light cream or milk. Dust with flour and leave until doubled in size. Dust over more flour and lightly press down the center of each roll. Bake at 425°F for 15 minutes. Place on a wire rack to cool, covered with a clean cloth, to give a soft crust.

French baguettes

Roll half the quantity of risen white bread dough into long cylinders. Leave to prove on a clean cloth, with the folds of the cloth between the dough. When doubled in size, roll the bread over on to greased baking sheets. Spray with salted water and make long slashes with a razor blade. Bake at 450°F for 20 minutes. Spray twice more during baking.

Porcupine rolls

Shape one third risen white dough into 14 teardrop shapes. Snip 'spines' into the rounded end. Push two currants into the pointed end. Place on greased baking sheets and leave until doubled in size. Brush with beaten egg and bake for 15 to 20 minutes at 450°F.

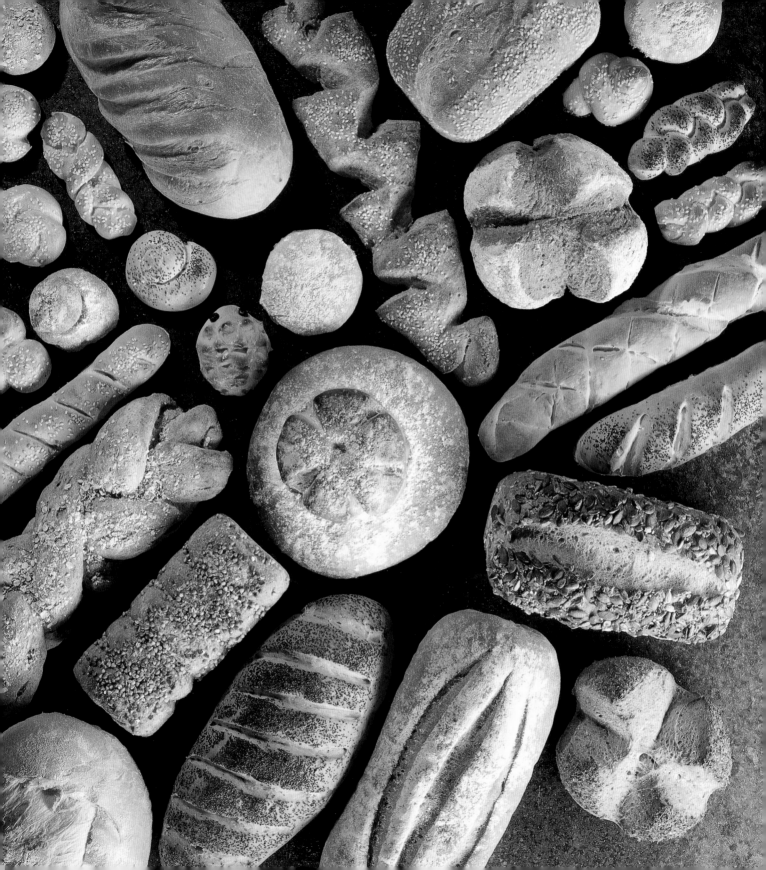

Country Breads

There's nothing more delicious than a hunk of honest, crusty, wholesome bread. These country bread recipes are very varied and use all sorts of grains.

Quick Wholewheat Bread

3 packages DRY YEAST

or

3 cakes FRESH YEAST

1 × 50 mg VITAMIN C TABLET (OPTIONAL)

1 tbsp. BROWN SUGAR

3 cups LUKEWARM WATER MADE BY MIXING TWO CUPS COLD WITH 1 CUP BOILING WATER

10 cups WHOLEWHEAT FLOUR

1 tbsp. SALT

3 tbsp. SOFT MARGARINE

Mix the dry or fresh yeast with the vitamin C tablet and 1 teaspoon of the sugar in a small bowl with 1 cup of the lukewarm water. Whisk together, then leave until frothy – about 10 minutes. Mix the flour, remaining sugar, salt and fat in a bowl. Pour in the yeast mixture and remaining water. Mix together then knead well. Divide and shape into loaves and rolls (see pages 16 to 17). Cover loosely with oiled plastic wrap and leave to rise in a warm place. Preheat the oven to 450°F. Grease three 8½ × 4¼ × 2¾ loaf pans or baking sheets. Bake loaves for 20 minutes, rolls for 8 minutes, turn oven down to 400°F and bake for 15 to 20 minutes longer.

MAKES 3 × 1 LB LOAVES

Cheese, Sage and Onion Braid

½ quantity QUICK WHOLEWHEAT BREAD DOUGH (SEE ABOVE)

1 large ONION, CHOPPED

2 tbsp. BUTTER

6 tbsp. MILK

2 tbsp. FRESH SAGE

or

1 tsp. DRIED SAGE

1 tsp. DRY MUSTARD

1 cup MOZZARELLA CHEESE, GRATED

1 tbsp. CRACKED WHEAT

Simmer the chopped onion in a small pan with the butter and milk for 5 minutes to soften. Drain and cool. Make the dough as above, then knead in the onion, sage, mustard and ½ cup of the cheese. Divide into three pieces and make each into a long sausage. Braid the three strands, pinching at ends to join firmly. Place on a greased baking sheet and cover with oiled plastic wrap. Leave to rise until doubled in size. Remove wrap and sprinkle with remaining ½ cup cheese and wheat. Preheat the oven to 450°F. Bake for 15 minutes, then turn down to 400°F and bake for 15 minutes longer.

MAKES 1 × 1½ LB LOAF

TOP: Cheese, Sage and Onion Braid
BOTTOM: Quick Wholewheat Bread

Oat and Honey Loaf

3 cups ROLLED OATS
1¼ cups MILK
1½ cups WHOLEWHEAT FLOUR
1½ cups ALL-PURPOSE FLOUR
2 packages QUICK-RISE YEAST
2 tsp. SALT
4 tbsp. MARGARINE
2 tbsp. HONEY
5 tbsp. LUKEWARM WATER

Place the oats and milk in a bowl and leave to soak for 30 minutes. Add all the other ingredients and mix to a soft dough.

Knead for 10 minutes until smooth. Replace in the bowl, cover with oiled plastic wrap and leave to rise until doubled in size. Knead the dough, to knock out the air.

Preheat the oven to 425°F. Shape the dough into a large and a small ball. Flatten out the large one and place on a greased baking sheet. Flatten the smaller one and make snips round the sides with scissors. Place on top of the large ball and press through the floured handle of a wooden spoon. Sprinkle with extra oats and bake for 25 minutes, or until the loaf sounds hollow when tapped underneath.   MAKES 1 × 1¼ LB LOAF

Rye Bread

2 packages DRY YEAST PLUS
1 tsp. SUGAR
or
2 cakes FRESH YEAST
⅔ cup LUKEWARM WATER
1 tsp. HONEY
1 tsp. MOLASSES
1½ cups ALL-PURPOSE FLOUR
3 cups RYE FLOUR
1 tsp. SALT
2 tbsp. CARAWAY SEEDS (OPTIONAL)
½ cup PLAIN YOGURT

Mix the dry yeast and sugar with the water and leave for 10 minutes until frothy, or blend the fresh yeast with the water. Stir in the honey and molasses.

Mix the flours and salt in a bowl, with the caraway seeds (if using). Add the yeast liquid and yogurt and mix to a soft dough. Turn onto a floured surface and knead until smooth for 5 minutes. Return to the bowl, cover with oiled plastic wrap and leave to rise until doubled in size. Knock back the dough and shape to a large round or place in a 9 × 5 × 3-inch pan. Prick the dough with a fork, cover again and prove for 35 minutes.

Preheat the oven to 400°F and bake the loaf for 45 minutes. Remove from the pan for the last 5 minutes. Place on a wire rack and cover with a dish cloth to cool.

MAKES 1 × 1¼ LB LOAF

TOP: *Oat and Honey Loaf*
BOTTOM: *Rye Bread*

Sourdough Bread

When you first make a sourdough you must allow plenty of time, as the starter and dough are made over four days to allow for long slow gentle rising. You will need to make the starter batter two days ahead. Sourdoughs are one of the oldest forms of leavened bread. Over the years they have been made by bakers in remote areas and by early pioneers who took on their travels a flour and water batter mixed with yeast. Part of the batter is used for baking and the rest is replenished and fed by adding flour and water. This happens every time the starter is used, so it will last as long as you need it.

Starter
2 packages DRY YEAST
2 cups LUKEWARM WATER
1 tsp. SUGAR
1⅔ cups WHOLEWHEAT FLOUR

Other ingredients
3⅓ cups WHOLEWHEAT FLOUR PLUS
3 cups ALL-PURPOSE FLOUR MIXED TOGETHER
1 tbsp. SALT
1 tbsp. SOFT BROWN SUGAR
1 tsp. BAKING SODA

Day 1: make the starter; dissolve the yeast in the water. Sprinkle in the sugar and leave for 10 minutes until frothy. Whisk in the flour, cover with a cloth, then leave at room temperature for 2 days. The starter will ferment and bubble, then die down to a flat grey liquid.

Day 3: sift 3 cups of the mixed flours, the salt, sugar and baking soda into a bowl. Add 1 cup of the starter. Mix well then cover with a cloth and leave to stand at room temperature for 24 hours.

When you have used 1 cup of the starter you will have to feed the remainder to keep it alive. Add equal amounts of flour and lukewarm water i.e. 1 cup water and 1 cup flour. Mix into the starter, stir well and refrigerate until needed.

Day 4: add the remaining flour and ¾ cup water to the mixture and knead well to form a soft dough. Roll into two balls and place on greased baking sheets. Cover with a damp cloth and leave to rise for 2 to 4 hours, until doubled in size.

Preheat the oven to 425°F. Brush the top with salted water glaze and with a razor, cut slashes across the tops. Bake for 8 minutes then turn down the heat to 400°F and bake for 35 minutes longer.   MAKES 2 × 1 LB LOAVES

Rye Sourdough Make the starter as above, but use 1¾ cups each of rye flour, strong white unbleached flour, and strong wholewheat flour to make up the dough. Prove and bake as above.

RIGHT: Sourdough Bread

Californian Raisin Bread

In California, bakers are using a paste made from raisins to enrich and moisten breads and cakes. This nutty tasting bread is based on an old American recipe called Squaw Bread. It is delicious served with soft cheeses like brie.

½ cup BOILING WATER
½ cup RAISINS
1 cake FRESH YEAST
or
1 package DRY YEAST
5¼ cups ALL-PURPOSE FLOUR
1 tsp. SALT
1 tbsp. VEGETABLE MARGARINE
2 tbsp. MILK
WHOLEWHEAT GRAINS TO FINISH

Pour the boiling water over the raisins and steep for 2 hours. Place in a food processor and blend to a thick paste. Mix the yeast with 1 cup lukewarm water. If using dry yeast, leave for 10 minutes until frothy. Place the flour and salt in a bowl, and rub in the fat until it resembles fine crumbs. Add the raisin paste with the lukewarm water mixture. Knead to a soft smooth dough for about 5 minutes, cover with oiled plastic wrap and leave until doubled in size. Knead again to knock out the air and shape into two large flat rounds. Place on oiled baking sheets and mark each round into four. Cover with oiled plastic wrap and leave until doubled. Brush with milk and sprinkle with the grains. Preheat the oven to 425°F. Bake for 20 minutes or until the bread sounds hollow when tapped. MAKES 2 × 12 OZ LOAVES

The Grant Loaf

Doris Grant originally wrote this recipe for a healthfood bread, making double the amount, in 1944. A legendary Scotswoman, married to the head of the Grant whisky family, she has spent most of her life campaigning against refined foods. Her bread is dense in texture, but has a delicious flavor and is so easy to make.

5 cups STONEGROUND 100% WHOLEWHEAT FLOUR
1 tsp. SALT
1 cake FRESH YEAST
or
1 package DRY YEAST
or
1 package QUICK-RISE YEAST
1 tsp. MOLASSES OR HONEY
2 cups LUKEWARM WATER

Stir the fresh or dry yeast with the molasses or honey, add ½ cup of the water and leave for 10 minutes to froth. If using quick-rise yeast, mix directly into the flour and salt and stir in the molasses with the water.

Sift the flour and salt together into a bowl. Pour in the yeast mixture, add the remaining water and mix well, by hand, working from the sides of the bowl to make a dough which feels elastic, and leaves the bowl clean. The dough will have a "slippery", slightly wet texture.

Place in a greased 9 × 5 × 3-inch loaf pan and leave to rise, covered with a damp dish cloth for 1 hour or until the dough has doubled. Preheat the oven to 400°F. Bake for 35 to 40 minutes or until the loaf sounds hollow when tapped. MAKES 1 × 2 LB LOAF

TOP: Californian Raisin Bread
BOTTOM: Grant Loaf

Pain de Campagne

A nutty tasting country loaf that keeps well. Serve it with soups or French cheeses.

1 cake FRESH YEAST
or
1 package DRY YEAST
6 cups UNBLEACHED ALL-PURPOSE FLOUR
or
1½ cups RYE FLOUR PLUS
4½ cups ALL-PURPOSE FLOUR, MIXED TOGETHER
1 tsp. SALT
2 tbsp. NATURAL BRAN
2 tbsp. WHEATGERM
2 tbsp. MARGARINE
1 tsp. MALT EXTRACT
½ cup PLAIN YOGURT

Measure 1 cup lukewarm water into a cup and sprinkle with the fresh or dried yeast. If using dried yeast, leave to reconstitute for 20 minutes.

Sift the flour and salt into a bowl and mix in the bran and wheatgerm. Rub in the margarine, add the yeast liquid with the malt extract and yogurt and mix to a soft dough. Knead for 5 minutes or until smooth and leave to rise in the bowl, covered in oiled plastic wrap, until doubled in size.

Knead again to knock out the air, then shape into a round and place on a greased and floured baking sheet.

Cover with oiled plastic wrap and leave until doubled in size. Sprinkle with flour and slash with a razor blade. Preheat the oven to 425°F and bake for 20 to 25 minutes or until bread sounds hollow when tapped.

MAKES 1 × 1½ LB LOAF

Mixed Seed Bread

½ quantity QUICK WHOLEWHEAT BREAD DOUGH (SEE PAGE 18)
½ cup PUMPKIN SEEDS, SHELLED
¼ cup SESAME OR POPPY SEEDS
½ cup SUNFLOWER SEEDS

Make up the wholewheat dough as directed on page 18 and knead until smooth. Knead in all the seeds until evenly distributed. Shape into two loaves and place in greased 8½ × 4¼ × 2¾-inch pans, slash down the center of each loaf with a sharp blade. Cover with oiled plastic wrap and leave until doubled in size.

Preheat the oven to 425°F. Bake the loaves for 20 minutes, then turn down the temperature to 400°F and bake for 15 minutes longer or until the bread sounds hollow when tapped. For a crispy crust all over, remove from the pans for the last 5 minutes.

MAKES 2 × 1 LB LOAVES

LEFT: Pain de Campagne
RIGHT: Mixed Seed Bread

Apricot and Honey Loaf

1 cake FRESH YEAST

or

1 package DRY YEAST

1 cup LUKEWARM MILK

1 EGG, BEATEN

1 tbsp. HONEY

2½ cups ALL-PURPOSE FLOUR

1⅔ cups WHOLEWHEAT FLOUR

1 tsp. SALT

2 tbsp. VEGETABLE MARGARINE

1⅓ cups DRIED APRICOTS, COARSELY CHOPPED

grated rind ½ ORANGE

2 tbsp. CHOPPED CANDIED PEEL (OPTIONAL)

⅓ cup NUTS, E.G. HAZELNUTS, ALMONDS
HALVED OR COARSELY CHOPPED

Blend the fresh yeast with ½ cup of the milk, or add the dry yeast and stand for 20 minutes. Whisk in the remaining milk, egg, and honey.

Sift the flours and salt into a bowl and rub in the fat. Add the yeast liquid and knead to a soft dough for 10 minutes. Replace in the bowl, cover with oiled plastic wrap and leave until doubled in size. Punch to knock out the air then knead in the apricots, orange rind, candied peel (if using) and nuts. Shape into two small loaves and place in 8½ × 4¼ × 2¾-inch greased pans. Cover with oiled plastic wrap and leave until doubled in size. Preheat the oven to 400°F. Bake for 40 to 45 minutes, until hollow when tapped.

MAKES 2 × 1 LB LOAVES

Walnut Breakfast Bread

Serve this delicious nutty bread with an egg and bacon breakfast, with soups and savories, or toasted for afternoon tea.

1 cake FRESH YEAST

or

1 package DRY YEAST

3⅓ cups WHOLEWHEAT FLOUR

1¼ cups ALL-PURPOSE FLOUR

1 tsp. SALT

2 tbsp. WALNUT OIL

½ cup SOUR CREAM

1 cup CHOPPED WALNUTS

BEATEN EGG TO GLAZE

Fill a measuring cup with 1 cup lukewarm water and sprinkle with the yeast. If using dry yeast leave to stand for 20 minutes until fothy. Place the flours and salt in a bowl and add the yeast liquid, walnut oil and sour cream. Knead to a soft dough for 5 minutes and replace in the bowl. Cover with oiled plastic wrap and leave until doubled in size. Lightly toast the walnut pieces, cool and chop coarsely. Knock out the air from the dough, then knead in the chopped nuts.

Shape into two loaves and place in greased 8½ × 4¼ × 2¾-inch pans. Leave until doubled in size. Preheat the oven to 400°F.

Brush with beaten egg, slash the tops with a razor blade, and bake for 30 to 40 minutes or until hollow when tapped.

MAKES 2 × 1 LB LOAVES

Top: Apricot and Honey Loaf
Bottom: Walnut Breakfast Bread

Enriched Breads

When you add butter, eggs or sugar to a plain dough, it is magically transformed from bread into a rich, light and airy feast. Adding spices, fruits and nuts makes breads even more special, turning them into mouth-watering traditional teatime treats.

Doughnuts

3¾ *cups* BREAD FLOUR

1 *tsp.* SALT

3 *tbsp.* GRANULATED SUGAR

1 *package* QUICK-RISE YEAST

1 *cup* LUKEWARM MILK

1 EGG, BEATEN

2 *tbsp.* BUTTER, MELTED

SUNFLOWER OIL FOR DEEP FAT FRYING

CONFECTIONER'S OR GRANULATED SUGAR FOR DUSTING

RASPBERRY JAM FOR FILLING

Place the flour, salt and sugar in a bowl with the dry yeast then beat in the milk, egg and butter. Knead for 10 minutes to make a soft, smooth dough. Replace in the bowl, cover, and leave until doubled in size, for about 2 hours.

Knock back the dough, then roll out to ¼ inch thick and cut out 18 circles, 4 inches in diameter, with a plain cutter. Place the rounds on oiled baking sheets and leave to prove until doubled in size, covered in oiled plastic wrap.

Heat oil in a deep fat fryer to 350°F or until a cube of bread browns in 1 minute. Fry the doughnuts for 5 minutes or until golden brown. Cool then dust in sugar in a plastic bag.

To fill, make a hole in the side of the cooled doughnut and pipe in a little raspberry jam.

For ring doughnuts, use the same method, but stamp out small rings from the center of each circle. Re-roll trimmings to use up all the dough. MAKES 18

RIGHT: Doughnuts

Chelsea Buns

Enriched dough

1 cake FRESH YEAST

or

1 package DRY YEAST

1 tsp. GRANULATED SUGAR

⅓ cup LUKEWARM MILK

2 cups ALL-PURPOSE FLOUR

½ tsp. SALT

2 tbsp. GRANULATED SUGAR

2 tbsp. BUTTER

1 EGG, BEATEN

Filling

2 tbsp. BUTTER, MELTED

1 cup MIXED DRIED FRUIT, COARSELY CHOPPED

½ tsp. ALLSPICE

¼ cup SOFT BROWN SUGAR

2 tbsp. HONEY

2 tbsp. GRANULATED SUGAR TO FINISH

Stir the yeast and sugar into the milk. If using dry yeast, leave to stand for 5 minutes. Mix in 7 tbsp. of the flour and leave until a frothy batter – about 20 minutes.

Sift together the remaining flour, salt and sugar and rub in the butter. Make a well and stir in the egg and yeast mixture and mix to a soft dough. Cover with oiled plastic wrap and leave for 1 hour until doubled in size.

Turn the risen dough onto a floured surface and roll out to a rectangle 12 × 9 inches. Brush with melted butter, combine spice and sugar, and sprinkle over dough with the fruit. Roll up, jelly-roll fashion, from the longest side. Cut into 9 equal pieces and place in a greased 8-inch square pan. Cover and leave to prove until doubled in size and the buns join together – about 40 minutes. Preheat the oven to 425°F. Bake for 10 minutes. Reduce heat to 350° and bake 15 to 20 minutes longer. Turn out of the pan, brush with the honey and sprinkle with granulated sugar.   MAKES 9

Sticky Fruit Couronne

This sweet yeasted ring is found in many forms in Scandinavian countries, enriched with dried peels, fruits and nuts.

1 quantity ENRICHED DOUGH (SEE ABOVE)

Filling

1 cup DRIED APRICOTS, CHOPPED

½ cup FRESH ORANGE JUICE

grated rind 1 ORANGE

6 tbsp. BUTTER

¼ cup SOFT LIGHT BROWN SUGAR

½ tsp. GROUND ALLSPICE

⅓ cup MIXED DRIED FRUIT, CHOPPED

⅓ cup GLACÉ CHERRIES, CHOPPED

⅓ cup ALMOND SLITHERS OR PECANS

2 tbsp HONEY

Make up the dough as above and leave to rise, covered, until doubled in size. Meanwhile place the apricots and orange juice in a pan, heat gently until the fruits absorb the juice, then cool.

Mix all the filling ingredients with the apricots. Roll out the dough to a rectangle 12 x 9 inches. Spread the filling evenly over the dough, then roll up from the long side, like a jelly roll. Cut in half lengthwise, twist the halves together, form in a ring, place on a greased baking sheet and leave, covered, for 1 hour until doubled in size.

Preheat oven to 400°F. Bake for 25 minutes until golden. Remove from oven and immediately brush the bread with honey. Cool on rack.   MAKES 1

LEFT: Sticky Fruit Couronne
RIGHT: Chelsea Buns

Bath Buns

1 quantity ENRICHED DOUGH (SEE PAGE 32)
¾ *cup* SEEDLESS RAISINS
3 *tbsp.* CANDIED PEEL
finely grated rind 1 LEMON
BEATEN EGG TO GLAZE
2 *tbsp.* GRANULATED SUGAR

Make up the dough, leave until doubled in size, then punch back. Knead in the raisins, peel and rind. Pull the dough into 12 rough pieces and place on a greased baking sheet. Brush with beaten egg and sprinkle with the sugar. Cover with oiled plastic wrap and leave to rise until doubled in size. Preheat the oven to 425°F. Bake for 15 minutes until golden brown.   MAKES 12

Irish Barm Brack

Traditionally baked in Ireland for Halloween, when it has a golden ring baked in it. Whoever gets the ring will be married within the year. Barm is the old word for the yeast liquid used to rise the brack.

1 cake FRESH YEAST
or
1 package DRY YEAST
1¼ *cups* LUKEWARM MILK
5 *cups* ALL-PURPOSE FLOUR
1 EGG, BEATEN
4 *tbsp.* BUTTER, MELTED
½ *tsp.* SALT
½ *tsp.* GROUND CINNAMON
pinch of GROUND NUTMEG
1½ *cups* SEEDLESS RAISINS
¾ *cup* CURRANTS
⅓ *cup* CANDIED PEEL, CHOPPED
¼ *cup* GRANULATED SUGAR

Place the yeast in a bowl and stir in the milk. Leave for 20 minutes if using dry yeast to reconstitute. Add 1 cup of the flour and whisk together. Leave to stand for 30 minutes or until frothy. Beat in the egg and butter, then sift in the remaining flour, salt and spices, and knead to a smooth soft dough. Knead in the fruits and sugar, cover with oiled plastic wrap and leave to rise for about 2 hours until doubled in size.

Knead the dough to knock out the air and place in a greased 8-inch springform cake pan. Leave covered with oiled plastic wrap until doubled in size.

Preheat the oven to 400°F. Bake for 30 to 40 minutes until the loaf is hollow when tapped. Cool and serve sliced and buttered. Toast any leftover brack and serve at teatime.   MAKES 1

TOP: Bath Buns
BOTTOM: Irish Barm Brack

Streusel-topped Coffee Bread

3¾ cups ALL-PURPOSE FLOUR
1 tsp. SALT
1 stick (½ cup) BUTTER
2 packages QUICK-RISE YEAST
¼ cup GRANULATED SUGAR
1⅓ cups DRIED APRICOTS, COARSELY CHOPPED
⅓ cup LARGE RAISINS
½ ORANGE, MINCED
2 EGGS, BEATEN
6 tbsp. LUKEWARM MILK

Topping
2 tbsp. BUTTER
¼ cup ALL-PURPOSE FLOUR
2 tbsp. GRANULATED SUGAR
1 tsp. GROUND CINNAMON

Sift the flour and salt into a bowl and rub in the butter. Stir in the yeast, sugar, dried fruits and orange.

Add the eggs and milk and beat well for 2 minutes. Place the mixture in a buttered 9 × 5 × 3-inch loaf pan or an 8-inch square cake pan. Cover with oiled plastic wrap and leave until doubled in size.

Preheat the oven to 400°F. Make the topping, rub the butter into the flour until it resembles fine crumbs, then stir in the sugar and cinnamon. Sprinkle over the top of the dough and bake for 40 to 50 minutes.   MAKES 1

Quick Breakfast Brioches

Buttery brioches are served for breakfast all over Europe. Leave this dough to rise overnight for a delicious breakfast treat.

2½ cups ALL-PURPOSE FLOUR
½ tsp. SALT
1 package QUICK-RISE YEAST
3 tbsp. MILK
6 tbsp. BUTTER, MELTED, COOLED
2 tbsp. GRANULATED SUGAR
2 EGGS, BEATEN
BEATEN EGG TO GLAZE

Mix the flour, salt and yeast together in a bowl, then add the remaining ingredients and mix to a sticky dough. Knead for 5 minutes, then return to the bowl and cover with oiled plastic wrap. Place in the refrigerator and leave to rise overnight.

Knock back the dough and divide into 12 pieces. Preheat the oven to 425°F and grease 12 brioche or deep muffin pans. Take a quarter from each piece of dough. Roll the dough into two balls, press the larger ball into the tin, press down with a finger to make a hole, then press the smaller one on top of the hole.

Brush with beaten egg, then leave to rise for 30 minutes until doubled in size and puffy. Bake for 15 minutes or until golden.   MAKES 12

TOP: *Streusel-topped Coffee Bread*
BOTTOM: *Quick Breakfast Brioches*

Kough-Aman

A rich buttery bread from Brittany with a delicious butterscotch crust on the base.

1 quantity ENRICHED DOUGH (SEE PAGE 32)
1 stick (8 tbsp.) BUTTER, SOFTENED
½ cup GRANULATED SUGAR

Make up the dough and leave to rise, covered, until doubled in size. Knock back the dough and roll out to a 10-inch square. Dab 6 tbsp. of the butter all over the dough, then sprinkle with 6 tbsp. of the sugar.

Fold the dough over into three, roll out again, keeping the butter inside. Roll three more times, then shape into an 8-inch round. Grease an 8-inch pan with the remaining butter and press in the dough. Leave in a warm place until doubled in size.

Preheat the oven to 425°F. Place the pan on a baking sheet and bake for 30 minutes. Sprinkle with the remaining sugar and leave to cool in the pan. MAKES 1

Sally Lunn

1 cake FRESH YEAST
or
1 package DRY YEAST
1 tbsp. CLEAR HONEY
1⅓ cups LUKEWARM MILK
3¾ cups ALL-PURPOSE FLOUR
1 tsp. SALT
finely grated rind 1 LEMON
2 EGGS, BEATEN
4 tbsp. BUTTER, MELTED

Glaze
1 tbsp. GRANULATED SUGAR DISSOLVED IN
2 tbsp. WATER

Stir the yeast and honey into the milk. If using dry yeast, leave to stand for 20 minutes until foaming.

Whisk in 1 cup of the flour and leave in a warm place until frothy, about 30 minutes. Add the remaining ingredients and beat to a smooth batter. Pour into two greased 8-inch layer cake pans and leave to rise until doubled in size for about 1½ hours. Preheat the oven to 425°F. Bake for 20 minutes or until light golden. Remove from the pans and cool. Boil the sugar and water together to a clear glaze and brush over the tops.

When cool cut horizontally into three. Sandwich together with whipped cream. MAKES 2

TOP: *Kough-Aman*
BOTTOM: *Sally Lunn*

Swedish Twists and Whirls

½ quantity DANISH PASTRY DOUGH (SEE PAGE 42)
6 tbsp. CHOCOLATE NUT SPREAD
1 GRAHAM CRACKER, CRUSHED
½ tsp. GROUND CINNAMON
½ cup PISTACHIOS OR MIXED CHOPPED NUTS

Roll dough out to a rectangle 12 × 5 inches. Mix all the filling ingredients together and spread thinly over the dough. Cut the dough in half lengthwise. Roll up one piece like a jelly roll, cut into ¼-inch thick slices and place on a baking sheet. Fold the remaining dough in half with the filling inside. Cut into ½-inch wide strips. Twist the strips and place on a baking sheet. Leave both pastries until puffy and bake as for Danish Pastries (see page 42) for 8 minutes.

MAKES 24

Pane d'Oro

This rich yellow bread is baked for special occasions in Italy.

2 cakes FRESH YEAST
or
2 packages DRY YEAST
6 EGG YOLKS
1 tsp. VANILLA
finely grated rind 1 LEMON
¼ cup GRANULATED SUGAR
3 cups ALL-PURPOSE FLOUR
½ tsp. SALT
1½ sticks (¾ cup) UNSALTED BUTTER, SOFTENED
CONFECTIONER'S SUGAR TO SPRINKLE

Place 3 tbsp. lukewarm water in a bowl and sprinkle with the yeast. If using dry yeast leave to stand for 15 minutes until frothy. Whisk in the egg yolks, rind, vanilla and sugar. Sift in 1¾ cups of the flour with the salt and mix to a soft batter. Keeping the batter in the bowl, beat in 10 tbsp. of the butter in pieces, adding the remaining flour as the dough gets sticky.

Knead until smooth and elastic, return to the bowl and cover with oiled plastic wrap. Leave until doubled in size, then punch back to knock out air. Melt the remaining butter and grease a fluted 8-inch brioche pan.

Place the dough in the pan and leave until doubled in size. Preheat the oven to 400°F.

Bake for 10 minutes, brush the top with the remaining butter and reduce the heat to 350°F. Bake for 30 minutes longer or until a toothpick inserted in the center comes out clean. Cool in the pan for 5 minutes, then turn out to cool on a wire rack. When cold, sprinkle with confectioner's sugar.

MAKES 1

TOP: Swedish Twists and Whirls
BOTTOM: Pane d'Oro

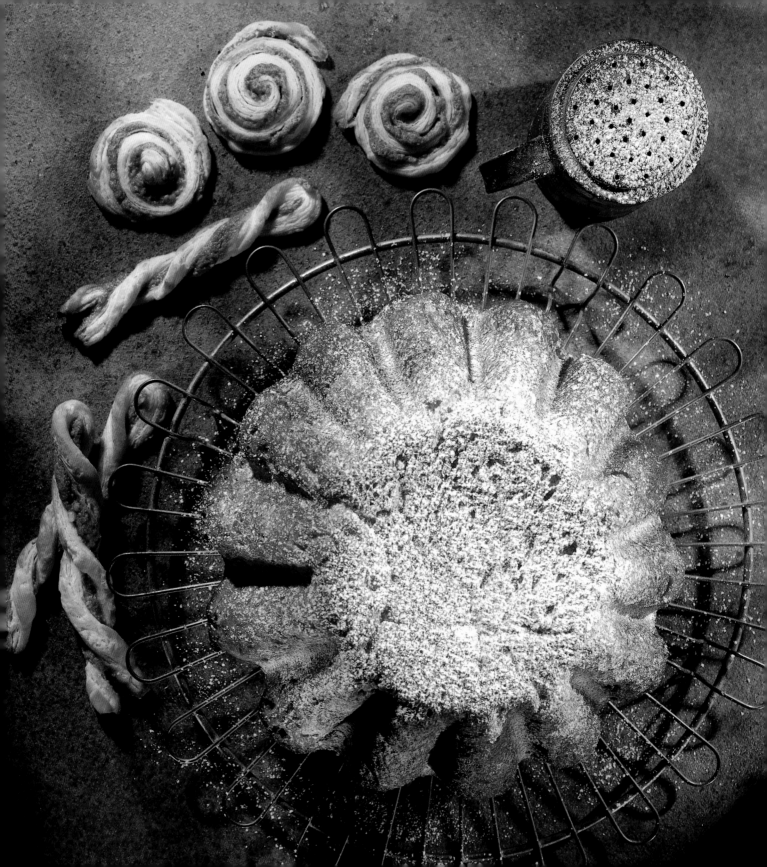

Continental Breads

The wealth of regional recipes from Europe is never ending, but here we have a selection of specialities from Italy, France, Denmark, and Germany, all deliciously different.

Danish Pastries

4 cups ALL-PURPOSE FLOUR
½ tsp. SALT
2½ sticks (1¼ cups) BUTTER
1 package QUICK-RISE YEAST
6 tbsp. GRANULATED SUGAR
¾ cup LUKEWARM WATER
2 EGGS, BEATEN
1 EGG WHITE, BEATEN, TO GLAZE

Decoration
1½ cups CONFECTIONER'S SUGAR
1 tsp. LEMON JUICE
GLACÉ CHERRIES OR FLAKED ALMONDS

Sift the flour and salt together. Cut 4 tbsp. of the butter into pieces and rub into the flour, then stir in the yeast and sugar. Add the water and eggs and mix to a soft dough. Knead for 5 minutes until smooth and elastic.

Place in an oiled plastic bag and chill in the refrigerator for 15 minutes. Cut the remaining butter into 16 thin slices and chill on a plate.

Halve the dough and roll each half into a rectangle 15 × 8 inches and place four slices of butter in the center. Fold one third of the dough over the butter and press down. Place four more slices on the folded dough and fold over the other third. Press down to seal. Give the dough a half turn, roll out to an oblong 16 × 6 inches, fold the ends into the center, press down and roll out and repeat again. Repeat with the remaining dough and

butter. Place in an oiled plastic bag and chill for 30 minutes. Repeat this rolling and chilling twice more, chilling for at least 2 hours in all.

Halve each piece of dough and shape as follows, leaving the shaped pastries on a baking sheet to rise for 20 minutes.

Preheat the oven to 400°F. Brush the shapes with beaten egg white and bake for 10 minutes. Reduce the heat to 350°F and bake 15 minutes longer. When cool, mix the confectioner's sugar with the lemon juice and drizzle over thinly. Decorate with glacé cherries or almonds.   MAKES 32

Windmills Mix 6 tbsp. ground almonds with 2 tbsp. lemon curd. Roll out a quarter of the dough to a rectangle 6 × 12 inches and cut into eight 3-inch squares. Make diagonal cuts from each corner to within ½ inch of the center. Place a little filling in the center of each square. Starting clockwise, fold each left-hand top corner into the center and seal.   MAKES 8

Cocks Combs Peel, core and slice 1 eating apple and cook to a pulp with 1 tsp. lemon juice and 1 tsp. of butter. Add 1 tsp. allspice and 3 tbsp. raisins. Roll a quarter of the dough into a rectangle 6 × 12 inches and cut into eight 3-inch squares. Spread the filling over half of each square to within ½ inch of the edges. Fold in half and slit edges in three places. Curve the pastry slightly.   MAKES 8

RIGHT: Danish Pastries

Focaccia

1 cake FRESH YEAST
1 cup LUKEWARM WATER
6 tbsp. OLIVE OIL
4¾ cups BREAD FLOUR
2 tsp. SALT
2 sprigs FRESH ROSEMARY, CHOPPED
1 tbsp. COARSE SEA SALT

Cream the yeast with half the water to a smooth liquid, then whisk in remaining water, and 4 tbsp. of the oil. Sift the flour and salt into a bowl and gradually add the yeast liquid to make a soft dough. Knead for 10 minutes until smooth. Leave to rise in the bowl covered with oiled plastic wrap for about 2 hours until doubled in size.

Knead to knock back the risen dough and knead in the rosemary.

Roll out and press the dough into a greased baking pan 10 × 14 inches. Cover with oiled plastic wrap and leave to prove until almost doubled. Dimple the dough by pressing fingertips into it to make ½-inch deep indentations.

Cover again and let rise until doubled. Preheat the oven to 425°F. Brush with the remaining oil and sprinkle with sea salt. Place a pan of hot water in the base of the oven. Bake the bread for 20 minutes until golden. Turn out to cool, but it is best eaten warm.

MAKES 1 × 1¼ LB LOAF

Olive Oil Bread with Sun-dried Tomatoes

1 quantity FOCACCIA DOUGH (SEE ABOVE)
½ cup CORNMEAL FLOUR
2 cups SUN-DRIED TOMATOES IN OIL, CHOPPED

Make up the dough. Drain oil from tomatoes and knead in the cornmeal flour with 2 tbsp. of the oil.

Leave the dough to rise, covered, until doubled. Knead out all the air. Knead half the chopped tomatoes into the dough, then roll out the dough and spread over the remainder. Roll up like a jelly roll and place in two oiled 8½ × 4¼ × 2¾-inch loaf pans. Leave until doubled, covered in oiled plastic wrap. Preheat the oven to 400°F. Slash the top with a sharp knife. Place a pan of hot water in the base of the oven. Bake the bread for 45 minutes. Turn out onto a wire rack to cool.

MAKES 2 × 1¼ LB LOAVES

Grissini

½ quantity QUICK WHOLEWHEAT DOUGH (SEE PAGE 18) MADE WITH HALF WHOLEWHEAT FLOUR, HALF ALL-PURPOSE FLOUR PLUS
3 tbsp. OLIVE OIL KNEADED INTO THE DOUGH

Preheat the oven to 450°F. Roll the dough out thinly to a rectangle 20 × 10 inches and cut into 36-40 strips ½ inch wide × 10 inches long. Roll the strips between the palms of your hands. Place on greased baking sheets and bake for 12 minutes until crisp. MAKES 36 TO 40

TOP LEFT: Grissini

TOP RIGHT: Olive Oil Bread with Sun-dried Tomatoes

BOTTOM: Focaccia

Pugilese

A delicious bread from Puglia in Italy with a crisp crust and a crumbly texture. You'll need to use whole fresh yeast for the authentic springy texture of both Pugilese and Ciabatta – but it's well worth it.

½ tsp. GRANULATED SUGAR
1¾ cups LUKEWARM WATER
1 cake FRESH YEAST
6 cups UNBLEACHED ALL-PURPOSE FLOUR
2 tsp. SALT
⅓ cup OLIVE OIL
1 cup (4 oz) GREEN OR BLACK OLIVES, PITTED AND
CHOPPED

Place the sugar in a cup with 4 tbsp. of the water, crumble in the yeast, and stir together. Mix the flour and salt together and pour in the yeast liquid with enough remaining water and olive oil to make a soft dough. Knead for 10 minutes until very soft and smooth. Knead in the olives, then return to the bowl and cover with oiled plastic wrap. Leave to rise for 3 hours or until doubled.

Gently turn the risen dough onto an oiled and floured baking sheet and tuck the edges under to make a round, but do not knead or knock out the air. Brush with salted water, then cover again with oiled plastic wrap and leave to prove until doubled in size. Preheat the oven to 425°F. Dust the dough with flour and bake for 10 minutes, then turn down the heat to 400°F and bake for 20 minutes longer or until the bread sounds hollow when tapped.   MAKES 1 × 1½ LB LOAF

Ciabatta

Serve Ciabatta with Italian soups and antipasti. It also makes deliciously substantial thick sandwiches, and toasts well. Put the spare bread in the freezer and serve it gently warmed through.

6 cups ALL-PURPOSE FLOUR
2 cakes FRESH YEAST
1¾ cups LUKEWARM WATER
7 tbsp. OLIVE OIL
2 tsp. SALT

Place 4 cups of the flour in a large bowl and make a well in the center. Mix the yeast with ⅓ cup of the water. Add enough of the water to the pint measure to bring the level up to 1½ cups. Pour the yeast liquid into the flour with remaining water and mix to make a very sticky dough. Beat with the flat of your hand until elastic, for about 5 minutes. Cover with oiled plastic wrap and leave to rise until doubled.

Knock back the dough and knead in the olive oil, 4 tbsp. water and salt. Knead in the remaining flour to make a soft dough. Replace in the bowl, cover again with oiled plastic wrap, and leave to rise until doubled in size. Divide the dough in the bowl and, without knocking back, turn the two pieces of dough out onto two greased and floured baking sheets. Pull the dough out to a long, oval shape. Leave to rise until doubled in size. Preheat the oven to 425°F. Sprinkle with flour and bake for 35 minutes.   MAKES 2 LOAVES

TOP: Pugilese
BOTTOM: Ciabatta

Pretzels

Called Salzbrezeln in Germany, few people realise these delicious bites are made from bread dough.

4 *cups* ALL-PURPOSE FLOUR
1 *tsp.* SALT
1 *package* QUICK-RISE YEAST
2 *tbsp.* SALTED BUTTER
1 *cup* MILK
1 EGG, BEATEN
COARSE SEA SALT TO FINISH

Mix the flour, salt and yeast in a bowl. Melt the butter then stir into the milk. When the liquid is lukewarm, pour into the flour and mix to a soft dough. Knead the dough well for 10 minutes until smooth. Divide the dough into 20 pieces. Roll each piece out to a 12-inch length. Tie the dough into a ring or knot. Place on greased baking sheets and leave to rise for 15 minutes or until puffy.

Preheat the oven to 450°F. Brush the pretzels with beaten egg then sprinkle liberally with coarse salt. Place in the oven and immediately reduce the temperature to 400°F and bake for 20 minutes or until dark and golden.

MAKES 20

Bagels

1 *cake* FRESH YEAST
or
1 *package* DRY YEAST
1 *cup* LUKEWARM MILK
1 *tsp.* GRANULATED SUGAR
3½ *cups* ALL-PURPOSE FLOUR
½ *tsp.* SALT
1 EGG, SEPARATED
4 *tbsp.* BUTTER, MELTED, COOLED
POPPY SEEDS, SESAME SEEDS, DRIED
ONION PIECES TO FINISH

Crumble the yeast into the milk and stir together with the sugar. If using dry yeast, leave to reconstitute for 10 minutes until frothy. Sift the flour and salt into a bowl. Whisk the egg white until frothy. Add the yeast liquid, melted butter and egg white to the flour and mix to a soft dough. Knead for 5 minutes until smooth and elastic.

Return to the bowl, cover with oiled plastic wrap and leave to rise for about 1½ hours or until doubled in size. Knock back the dough and divide into 16 pieces. Roll each piece about 6 inches long. Join and form into a neat ring. Arrange the rings on oiled baking sheets, cover with a dry cloth and leave to rise until doubled in size.

Preheat the oven to 400°F. Bring a large pan of water to the boil, then turn down the heat so it is just simmering. Drop the bagels into the water three at a time for 20 seconds. Scoop out with a perforated spoon and place on oiled baking sheets. Beat the egg yolk with 1 tbsp. water and brush the glaze over the bagels.

Sprinkle with seeds or onion pieces. Bake for 20 minutes or until golden brown.

Serve split, with cream cheese and smoked salmon.

MAKES 14 TO 16

TOP: Pretzels
BOTTOM: Bagels

Kugelhopf

double quantity ENRICHED DOUGH (SEE PAGE 32)
½ cup WHOLE ALMONDS IN SKINS
grated rind 1 LEMON
1 tsp. VANILLA
4 oz SWEET COOKING CHOCOLATE, CHOPPED
⅔ cup RAISINS
2 tbsp. DARK RUM
CONFECTIONER'S SUGAR TO SPRINKLE

Make up a double quantity of enriched dough, leave to rise until doubled, then knead to knock out the air. Thickly butter the inside of an 8-inch Kugelhopf mold. Press the almonds around the sides, then chill in the refrigerator.

Knead the lemon zest, vanilla, chocolate, raisins and rum into the dough. Carefully place the dough into the mold, trying not to displace the almonds. Leave to prove for 1 hour or until doubled in size. Preheat the oven to 400°F. Bake for 45 minutes or until a toothpick inserted into the center comes out clean. Cool for 5 minutes, then turn out onto a wire rack. Sprinkle with confectioner's sugar when cool.   MAKES 1

Croissants

1 quantity DANISH PASTRY DOUGH (SEE PAGE 42)
MADE WITHOUT SUGAR

Glaze
1 EGG, BEATEN
1 tbsp. WATER

Roll and chill the dough as for Danish Pastries, then finally roll out to a rectangle 22 × 13 inches. Halve lengthwise and cut each strip into 18 triangles.

Brush glaze over the triangles then roll up loosely, towards the point. Place well apart on greased baking sheets and curve into crescents, cover with oiled plastic wrap and leave to prove for 30 minutes or until puffy. Preheat the oven to 450°F. Brush with glaze again, and bake for 15 to 20 minutes.   MAKES 18

Pains au Chocolat Roll out the dough and cut into 18 oblongs measuring about 4 × 6 inches. Using 8 oz (2 × 4 oz bars) sweet cooking chocolate, place two squares of chocolate on one short end of the oblong, and roll the dough loosely over to make a cylinder. Place on a greased baking sheet and glaze. Leave, covered with oiled plastic wrap for 30 minutes until puffy, then glaze and bake.

Top: Kugelhopf
Bottom: Croissants

Savarin

2 cakes FRESH YEAST

or

2 packages DRY YEAST

6 tbsp. LUKEWARM MILK

2 cups ALL-PURPOSE FLOUR

½ tsp. SALT

2 tbsp. GRANULATED SUGAR

3 EGGS, BEATEN

1 stick (½ cup) BUTTER, SOFTENED

finely grated rind 1 ORANGE

Syrup

1 cup GRANULATED SUGAR

½ cup ORANGE JUICE

½ cup WATER

2 tbsp. BRANDY

5 tbsp. APRICOT JAM, SIEVED

Crumble the yeast into a bowl and stir in the milk. If using dry yeast, leave for 10 minutes to reconstitute. Stir in ½ cup of the flour and whisk together.

Leave in a warm place for about 20 minutes until frothy. Brush a 9-inch savarin or ring mold with melted butter. Stir the remaining flour with the salt, sugar, beaten eggs, softened butter and orange zest and beat together for 4 to 5 minutes or until smooth and glossy. Half fill the mold with the batter and place in a large oiled plastic bag until doubled in size – about 40 minutes.

Preheat the oven to 400°F. Bake for 30 to 35 minutes, then turn out onto a wire rack to cool. When cold, prick all over with a toothpick.

Make the syrup: place the sugar, orange juice and 1 tbsp. of the water in a saucepan, heat gently until the sugar dissolves. Add the remaining water and boil until reduced by half and thickened. Stir in the brandy. Place a tray under the rack and spoon the syrup over the cake until completely absorbed. Brush with apricot glaze, and fill the center with fresh fruit to serve.   MAKES 1

Babas

1 quantity SAVARIN BATTER (SEE ABOVE)

Syrup

¾ cup HONEY

½ cup WATER

3 tbsp. DARK RUM

Grease twelve 3-inch baba molds. Make up the batter and half fill the molds with the mixture. Cover and leave to rise until the molds are about two-thirds full, about 25 minutes. Preheat the oven to 400°F. Bake for 10 to 15 minutes until golden.

Cool in the molds then turn out onto a wire rack. Prick all over, then warm the syrup ingredients together and brush over the babas. Decorate with whipped cream and glacé cherries or with fresh fruit.   MAKES 12

TOP: Babas

BOTTOM: Savarin

Breads from the British Isles

Recipes for regional English, Welsh, Irish and Scottish breads have travelled all over the world and you'll come across these traditional bakes in the most unlikely places. With the variety of so many breads it is difficult to choose, but here is a selection of the most popular favorites .

Lardy Cake

Lardy cake is rich and sticky – serve it upside down, as a delicious toffee layer forms underneath.

4 cups ALL-PURPOSE FLOUR
1 tbsp. LARD OR WHITE VEGETABLE
SHORTENING
1 tsp. SALT
1 package QUICK-RISE YEAST
1 cup LUKEWARM WATER
6 tbsp. HONEY FOR GLAZING

Filling
¾ cup GRANULATED SUGAR
1 cup plus 2 tbsp. MIXED DRIED FRUIT, COARSELY CHOPPED
1 tsp. ALLSPICE
½ cup LARD OR WHITE VEGETABLE
SHORTENING

Rub the fat into the flour and salt until it resembles fine crumbs. Sir in the yeast and the water and mix to a soft dough. Knead for 5 to 6 minutes until smooth, then leave to rise in an oiled plastic bag for about 1 hour until doubled. Knead to punch out the air.

Mix the sugar, dried fruit and spice together. Roll out the dough to an oblong ½ inch thick. Dot one third of the lard over the bottom two thirds of the dough, then sprinkle a third of the filling over the fat.

Fold the bottom plain third up over the middle third, then fold the other third down over it. Give the dough a quarter turn then repeat the folding and rolling twice more until all the fat and filling is incorporated. Roll out the dough to fit a greased 9-inch square baking pan. Use a very sharp knife to slash the top into diamonds.

Cover and leave to double in size. Preheat the oven to 400°F. Bake for 30 to 35 minutes or until golden. Lift the cake onto a wire rack and brush with the honey. Serve warm cut into thick slices.   MAKES 1

RIGHT: Lardy Cake

Buttery Aberdeen Rowies

½ quantity TRADITIONAL WHITE BREAD DOUGH
(SEE PAGE 14)
½ cup BUTTER
½ cup WHITE VEGETABLE SHORTENING

Make up a half batch of white bread dough using 6 cups flour. Cover with oiled plastic wrap and leave to rise until doubled in size.

Mash the butter and shortening together, knock back the dough and roll out to an oblong. Dab two thirds of the dough with one third of the fat. Fold over the plain section of dough, then fold over to make a sandwich.

Press down the edges, then chill for 30 minutes. Give the dough a half turn, roll out and add another third of the fat. Chill, roll, and repeat with the remaining fat.

Preheat the oven to 400°F. Roll out the dough and stamp out 20 rounds using a 3-inch cutter. Place on baking sheets and fold over. Leave to puff up for 20 minutes, then bake for 20 to 25 minutes until golden.

MAKES 20

Bara Brith

Serve this delicious speckly spiced bread from North Wales sliced and buttered, or toast any left over the next day.

4 cups BREAD FLOUR
1 tsp. SALT
1 tsp. ALLSPICE
6 tbsp. MARGARINE
1 package QUICK-RISE YEAST
½ cup SOFT DARK BROWN SUGAR
½ cup LUKEWARM MILK
½ cup COLD TEA
1 EGG, BEATEN
2¼ cups MIXED DRIED FRUIT, COARSELY CHOPPED
⅓ cup MIXED CHOPPED PEEL

Glaze
¼ cup GRANULATED SUGAR DISSOLVED WITH
1 tbsp. WATER

Sift the flour, salt and spice into a bowl and rub in the vegetable fat until the mixture resembles fine crumbs.

Mix in the yeast and sugar, make a well and add the milk, tea and beaten egg. Knead to a sticky dough for 5 minutes, then knead in the dried fruit and peel.

Cover with oiled plastic wrap and leave to rise until doubled in size. Knock back and knead well then place in an 8-inch greased springform pan or a 9 × 5 × 3-inch loaf pan. Leave, covered in oiled plastic wrap, until doubled in size again.

Preheat the oven to 425°F. Bake for 10 minutes then reduce the heat to 375°F and bake for 25 minutes longer. Turn out of the pan after 4 minutes, then brush with the glaze.

MAKES 1 × 2 LB LOAF

TOP: Buttery Aberdeen Rowies
BOTTOM: Bara Brith

English Muffins

1 cake FRESH YEAST

or

1 package DRY YEAST

1 cup LUKEWARM MILK

4 cups ALL-PURPOSE FLOUR

1 tsp. SALT

1 EGG, BEATEN

2 tbsp. BUTTER, MELTED

½ cup FINE GROUND SEMOLINA

Stir the yeast into the milk. If using dry yeast leave until frothy for 15 minutes. Sift the flour and salt together, add the yeast liquid, egg and butter, and mix to a soft dough. Knead well until smooth, elastic and no longer sticky. Return to the bowl, cover with oiled plastic wrap and leave until doubled in size.

Turn out the dough and roll out to a ½-inch thickness. Cut into 3⅓-inch plain rounds, dust all over with the semolina and place on a floured baking sheet. Cover and leave to prove until doubled in size.

Either cook the muffins on a griddle for 5 minutes each side as for crumpets, or bake in a preheated oven at 450°F for 10 minutes, turning over after 5 minutes.

To serve, toast on both sides, pull apart with a fork and butter.

MAKES 20

Crumpets

1 package DRY YEAST

or

1 cake FRESH YEAST

1 tsp. GRANULATED SUGAR

1 cup LUKEWARM WATER

3 cups ALL-PURPOSE FLOUR

½ tsp. BAKING SODA

1 tsp. SALT

1 cup LUKEWARM MILK

Stir the yeast and sugar into the water. If using dry yeast, stand for 10 minutes to reconstitute. Whisk in the flour and leave for 30 minutes until light and frothy.

Gradually beat in remaining ingredients until smooth. Add more milk if necessary to make a pouring batter.

Lightly grease a clean griddle and 3-inch plain crumpet rings or cutters. If you don't have a griddle, use a heavy-based skillet. Heat the griddle or skillet and place the greased rings on top. Pour 2 tbsp. batter into each ring. Cook until set and holes burst out on top. Remove from the rings and turn over to lightly brown. Repeat using remaining batter. Cool on a wire rack and serve toasted and buttered.

MAKES 20

TOP AND RIGHT: Muffins

LEFT: Crumpets

Soda Bread

In Ireland, soda bread is made with buttermilk, which gives an authentic tangy taste and soft moist texture.

2 cups ALL-PURPOSE FLOUR
2 cups WHOLEWHEAT FLOUR
1 tsp. SALT
1 tsp. BAKING SODA
1 tbsp. BAKING POWDER
1 tsp. VEGETABLE OIL
⅔ cup PLAIN YOGURT OR BUTTERMILK
⅔ cup LUKEWARM WATER

Preheat the oven to 400°F. Sift the flours, salt and rising agents together into a bowl and mix in the bran from the sieve. Add the oil and yogurt with lukewarm water and mix to a soft dough. Divide into two pieces and roll each piece into a ball. Place on a greased baking sheet, dust with flour and cut a deep cross in the middle of each round. Bake for 30 minutes.   MAKES 2 × 10 OZ LOAVES

Cornish Saffron Bread

½ tsp. SAFFRON STRANDS
2 cakes FRESH YEAST
or
2 packages DRY YEAST
½ tsp. GRANULATED SUGAR
⅔ cup LUKEWARM MILK
4 cups ALL-PURPOSE FLOUR
1 tsp. SALT
1 stick (½ cup) BUTTER
finely grated rind 1 LEMON
2 tbsp. SOFT BROWN SUGAR
1 cup CURRANTS

Place the saffron in a bowl and pour on ½ cup boiling water. Leave for 2 hours to infuse.

Stir the yeast and sugar into the milk. If using dry yeast, leave to reconstitute for 15 minutes until frothy. Sift the flour and salt into a bowl, rub in the butter until it resembles fine crumbs, then stir in the lemon rind and brown sugar. Strain in the saffron infusion and add the yeast liquid. Beat well, in a mixer if possible, then mix in the currants. Place the dough in a greased 8-inch round springform pan, cover with oiled plastic wrap and leave to rise until doubled.

Preheat the oven to 400°F. Bake for 30 minutes, then turn down the heat to 350°F and bake for 20 minutes longer or until golden on top and hollow sounding when tapped. Cool on a wire rack and serve sliced and buttered.   MAKES 1 × 1½ LB LOAF

LEFT: Soda Bread
RIGHT: Cornish Saffron Bread

American Breads

New styles of baking are found in America. Many breads here are still influenced by the early settlers who cooked from covered wagons on the trail, and also by the Latin Americans.

Johnny Cake

This cornbread made by the early Pioneers, was possibly named Journey Bread as it was made on the trail, or after the Shawnee tribe who made similar breads. Serve Johnny Cake hot for breakfast or brunch, it is deliciously crisp on the outside but soft inside.

1¾ *cups* FINE CORNMEAL
1¾ *cups* ALL-PURPOSE FLOUR
1 *tbsp.* BAKING POWDER
1 *tsp.* SALT
1 *tbsp.* GRANULATED SUGAR
6 *tbsp.* SOFT MARGARINE
2 *cups* MILK

Preheat the oven to 350°F. Grease a 9-inch square pan.

Sift the cornmeal, flour, baking powder, salt and sugar together, then lightly rub in the margarine until the mixture resembles fine crumbs. Mix in the milk and beat to a smooth batter. Pour into the pan and bake for 30 minutes or until a toothpick inserted in the center comes out clean. Cut into squares and serve hot, buttered.

MAKES 1

Cornmeal Muffins and Corn Husks

1 *cup* ALL-PURPOSE FLOUR
1 *tsp.* SALT
4 *tsp.* BAKING POWDER
3 *tbsp.* GRANULATED SUGAR
1 *cup* FINE CORNMEAL
2 EGGS, BEATEN
1 *cup* MILK
2 *tbsp.* BUTTER, MELTED
1 *tbsp.* CARAWAY SEEDS OR CHOPPED FRESH CHIVES

Preheat the oven to 400°F. Sift the flour, salt, baking powder, sugar and cornmeal together.

Add the eggs, milk and melted butter, and beat well to make a smooth mixture. Beat in the caraway seeds or chives.

Pour into a greased 12-hole deep muffin pan or 10 husk molds. Bake muffins for 15 to 20 minutes and cornbreads for 25 minutes. MAKES 12 MUFFINS OR 10 CORN HUSKS

LEFT: Johnny Cake

TOP AND RIGHT: Cornmeal Muffins and Corn Husks

Zucchini Bread

1½ cups ALL-PURPOSE FLOUR
¾ cup SOFT BROWN SUGAR
2 tsp. BAKING POWDER
½ tsp. SALT
¾ cup WALNUT PIECES, CHOPPED
2 EGGS, BEATEN
⅓ cup SUNFLOWER OIL
1½ cups ZUCCHINI, GRATED
1 tsp. ORANGE OR LEMON RIND

Grease an 8½ × 4¼ × 2¾-inch loaf pan. Preheat the oven to 350°F.

Sift the flour, sugar, baking powder and salt into a bowl and add the walnuts. Beat the eggs and oil together, then mix into the bowl with the zucchini and rind. Mix quickly together, spoon into the pan and bake for 50 minutes.

Leave to cool in the pan for 5 minutes, then turn out. Serve sliced and buttered.   MAKES 1 × 1½ LB LOAF

Tortillas

Serve tortillas with spicy Mexican foods. Make a batch for the freezer for a buffet party.

4 cups ALL-PURPOSE FLOUR
1 tsp. SALT
6 tbsp. LARD OR WHITE VEGETABLE
SHORTENING
1 cup WARM WATER

Sift the flour and salt into a bowl, and rub in the lard. Add enough warm water to give a soft, slightly sticky dough.

Knead on a lightly floured surface until no longer sticky. Divide the dough into 6 and roll the first piece very thinly. Cut out as many 5-inch circles as possible, using a plate as a guide. Repeat with the remaining dough, then knead the trimmings together, roll and cut out more tortillas.

Heat a non-stick skillet or griddle, and dry fry each tortilla for 40 seconds per side. They should be soft, with a few brown bubbles. Don't overcook or they will become brittle. Stack the tortillas and cover with a clean cloth, serve warm. To keep, stack with a disc of greaseproof paper between them, wrap in a plastic bag, store in the refrigerator for 2 days. To freeze, stack and pack as above in airtight bags and keep for up to 6 months. To serve, reheat at 375°F for 15 minutes.

MAKES ABOUT 36

LEFT: Zucchini Bread
RIGHT: Tortillas

Anadama Bread

Anadama bread is one of the earliest traditional American breads. There is no consistent explanation of this peculiar name.

1 cup MILK AND WATER, MIXED
½ cup FINE CORNMEAL
3 tbsp. BUTTER, SOFTENED
¼ cup MOLASSES
1 tsp. SALT
1 package DRY YEAST
½ cup LUKEWARM WATER
2½ cups UNBLEACHED ALL-PURPOSE FLOUR
1¾ cup WHOLEWHEAT FLOUR

Bring the milk to just below boiling point, then stir in the cornmeal, butter, molasses and salt. Set aside to cool.

Sprinkle the dry yeast into the water and leave until frothy for about 20 minutes. Add the yeast liquid to the cornmeal mixture with enough flour to make a sticky dough. Knead well for 5 minutes, scraping the mixture up and re-kneading it, as it is sticky. Place in an oiled bowl, cover with oiled plastic wrap and leave to rise for 1 hour, or until doubled in size.

Punch back the dough to knock out all the air, then place in an oiled 9 × 5 × 3-inch loaf pan. Cover with oiled plastic wrap and leave to prove until almost doubled. Preheat the over to 400°F. Slash the top, then bake for 15 minutes, turn down the heat to 350°F and bake for 30 minutes longer, until hollow when tapped. Remove from the pan for the last 5 minutes of baking.

MAKES 1 × 2 LB LOAF

Parker House Rolls

These rolls, created for the well-known nineteenth-century Parker House Hotel in Boston, are famous for their unique folds and delicate flavor.

½ quantity TRADITIONAL WHITE BREAD DOUGH
(SEE PAGE 14) ENRICHED WITH
3 tbsp. BUTTER (INSTEAD OF LARD) AND
1 tbsp. HONEY (INSTEAD OF GRANULATED
SUGAR)
1 EGG, BEATEN
¼ cup BUTTER, MELTED

Make up the yeast liquid, then add to the flour with the honey and egg. Knead for 5 minutes to a soft, smooth dough. Cover with oiled plastic wrap and leave to rise for 1 hour or until doubled in size. Knock back the dough to punch out all the air.

Roll the dough out to ½-inch thickness. Cut out into 3 inch rounds. Press the dull side of a knife across the center of each roll. Brush the rounds with some of the melted butter, then fold over across the center. Place on greased baking sheets, then brush the tops with the remaining melted butter. Leave to rise for 40 minutes until puffy.

Meanwhile, preheat the oven to 425°F. Bake for 15 to 20 minutes until light golden. Serve warm. MAKES 30

TOP: *Anadama Bread*
BOTTOM: *Parker House Rolls*

Eastern Breads

Freshly made flat breads are the staple of many Eastern countries, where they are eaten with curries or vegetable dishes. They add that authentic touch to exotic spicy feasts.

Chapatis

1⅔ *cups* WHOLEWHEAT FLOUR
½ *cup* WATER
1 *tsp.* SALT

Sift the flour into a bowl and discard most of the coarse pieces of bran. Add half the water, then the salt and mix together. Gradually add the remaining water and mix to a sticky dough. Turn out onto a floured surface and knead until smooth and elastic, but still slightly moist. Pull off small pieces of dough, roll in flour and flatten into a disc with your palm. Press out the disc, then roll out thinly to a circle about 7 inches in diameter. Heat a heavy-based skillet, but do not add any fat. Dry fry the chapati for 30 seconds on each side until speckled brown and puffy. Turn over, press the chapati down on the pan with a clean cloth for 30 seconds, then turn over and repeat. Keep warm in a clean cloth while frying the remaining chapatis.   MAKES 10

For pooris, make up a batch of chapati dough and roll out as above, but make them smaller, about 4 inches in diameter. Heat a deep skillet full of oil until it reaches 375°F. Drop each poori into the oil, fry until puffed up then turn over with tongs and cook the other side. Drain on paper towels and keep warm as above. Serve immediately.   MAKES 12 TO 14

Parathas

1 *quantity* CHAPATI DOUGH (SEE ABOVE)
¾ *cup* CLARIFIED BUTTER

Make up the chapati dough and roll into 6-inch circles. Brush each circle with 2 tsp. clarified butter, then fold over, then up to make a parcel. Dip the folded dough in flour and roll out to a 7-inch round.

Heat a griddle or heavy-based skillet and brush with 1 tsp. butter.

Fry each paratha on both sides until crisp and puffy. Serve immediately.   MAKES 15

Top: Chapatis and Parathas
Bottom: Pooris

Blinis

1 cake FRESH YEAST
1 tsp. GRANULATED SUGAR
¾ cup LUKEWARM WATER
¾ cup BUCKWHEAT FLOUR AND
½ cup ALL-PURPOSE FLOUR
or
1¼ cups BREAD OR ALL-PURPOSE FLOUR
1 tsp. SALT
1 EGG, SEPARATED
¾ cup (6 fl oz) MILK
1 tbsp. SOUR CREAM
2 tbsp. BUTTER

Mix the yeast with the sugar and water and leave to reactivate and froth. Sift the flours and salt into a bowl. Whisk in the the egg yolk and yeast liquid, to make a thick batter. Cover the bowl with a dish cloth and leave to double in size for 1 to 2 hours. Whisk in the milk and sour cream, then beat the egg white until stiff, and gently fold into the batter. Leave for 30 minutes until frothy. Heat a griddle or heavy-based skillet and lightly grease with the butter. Spoon 3 tbsp. mixture onto the griddle to make a small pancake. Cook for 2 to 3 minutes, then turn the blini over and cook the other side. Keep warm while cooking the remaining batter. Serve warm with sour cream and cod's roe.

MAKES 10 TO 12

Pitas

½ quantity TRADITIONAL WHITE BREAD DOUGH (SEE PAGE 14)

Make up the bread dough, knead well and leave to rise until doubled in size, covered with oiled plastic wrap. Preheat the oven to 450°F.

Knead the dough to knock out any large air bubbles then divide into 10 equal pieces. Knead each one lightly then shape into a smooth ball. Roll out each ball to a ¼-inch thick oval shape and leave to prove until the shapes become puffy.

Heat 2 oiled baking sheets, place 2 to 3 ovals on each sheet and bake for about 10 minutes until light golden.

Cool on a wire rack while cooking the rest. Halve and split the pitas and serve filled with Greek salad and kebabed meats.

MAKES 10

TOP: Blinis

BOTTOM: Pitas

Festive Breads

Many countries have their own special breads for celebrations like Christmas, Easter, the Sabbath or harvest time. Lovingly prepared with the best butter, eggs, spices and fruits, they are a symbol of peace and plenty.

St. Lucia Breads

1 quantity ENRICHED DOUGH (SEE PAGE 32)
⅔ cup CURRANTS
1 EGG, BEATEN

Divide the dough into 1 oz pieces, roll into 8-inch sausages, and shape as follows:

For 'S' shapes roll each end in an opposite direction to meet in the center.

For ram's horns fold the strip in half then roll each end back a couple of turns.

For crossed 'S' shapes divide the strip in 2, cross to make an 'X' then roll each end into an 'S' shape.

For back-to-back 'C' shapes divide the strip in 2, curl into 'C's and press together.

For bishop's wig divide the strip into 3 strands, roll up the ends and press together.

Arrange on greased baking sheets, decorate with the currants and brush with the beaten egg. Preheat the oven to 400°F and bake for 10 to 15 minutes until golden.

MAKES 18

Stollen

No Christmas in Germany would be complete without a Stollen. Served sliced, it is light and fruity and fragrant with a tang of lemons.

1 quantity ENRICHED DOUGH (SEE PAGE 32)
¼ cup SLIVERED ALMONDS
Grated rind of 1 LEMON
1 cup MIXED DRIED FRUIT
⅓ cup GLACÉ CHERRIES, CHOPPED
2 tbsp. BUTTER, MELTED
¾ cup ALMOND PASTE
½ cup CONFECTIONER'S SUGAR

Leave the dough to rise, covered in oiled plastic wrap, until doubled. Knead to knock out the air, then gradually work in the nuts, fruit and lemon rind. Shape the dough into an oval 9 × 12 inches and place on a greased baking sheet. Brush the surface with some of the melted butter. Shape the almond paste into a 9-inch long sausage, place down the center of the dough, fold one side over the almond paste, then the other flap over this. Brush with remaining melted butter, cover with plastic wrap and leave 1 hour until doubled in size.

Preheat the oven to 400°F. Bake for 30 to 40 minutes then cool and sprinkle with sugar.

MAKES 1

LEFT: St. Lucia Breads
RIGHT: Stollen

Bishop's Bread

½ cup GLACÉ CHERRIES, WASHED, HALVED

⅓ cup DRIED FIGS, CHOPPED

⅔ cup GLACÉ PINEAPPLE, CHOPPED

2 tbsp. CRYSTALLIZED ANGELICA, WASHED, CHOPPED

1 cup LARGE CALIFORNIA RAISINS

½ cup PECAN NUTS

⅓ cup WHOLE ALMONDS IN SKINS

½ cup WALNUT HALVES

½ cup SHELLED BRAZIL NUTS

1¼ cups ALL-PURPOSE FLOUR

PINCH OF SALT

1 tsp. BAKING POWDER

3 EGGS

½ cup DARK BROWN SUGAR

4 to 5 tbsp. BRANDY

Preheat the oven to 375°F. Butter a 10 × 5 × 3-inch loaf pan. Toss the fruit and nuts in a little of the flour then sift the remaining flour into a bowl with the salt and baking powder. Add the fruit and nuts and mix well.

Whisk the eggs and sugar together until thick and creamy. Mix into the fruit and nuts to make a stiff mixture. Spoon into the pan and level the top. Bake for about 1¾ hours or until firm and golden. Spoon over the brandy while still hot then leave to cool in the pan.

Keeps in an airtight tin for up to 3 weeks.   MAKES 1

Fougasses

Fougasse forms the center of the traditional 13 desserts served after the Christmas Eve meal in Provence. These can be any combination of three fresh fruits, three nuts, three dried fruits and sweetmeats like nougat or crystallized fruits.

6 cups ALL-PURPOSE FLOUR

1 tsp. SALT

¾ cup GRANULATED SUGAR

1 cake FRESH YEAST

2 EGGS, BEATEN

Grated rind 1 LARGE ORANGE

1 tbsp. WATER

5 tbsp. OLIVE OIL

½ cup WHOLE CANDIED ORANGE PEELS, CHOPPED

Mix the flour, salt and sugar together in a large bowl. Crumble the yeast into a bowl containing ⅓ cup lukewarm water. Leave for 5 minutes then add 6 tbsp. of the flour and mix to a thick batter. Leave to stand for 15 minutes until spongy. Beat the eggs, orange rind and oil together. Add to the remaining flour with the yeast batter to make a soft dough. Knead for 10 minutes until smooth and elastic, then knead in the chopped peels. Divide into 4 pieces. Roll each into an oval about ½ inch thick and 12 × 6 inches.

Make slashes with a knife to make a herringbone design. Arrange the ovals on greased baking sheets and leave to rise, covered with oiled plastic wrap, until doubled in size.

Preheat the oven to 400°F. Brush lightly with oil and bake for 20 minutes.   MAKES 4

LEFT: Bishop's Bread

RIGHT: Fougasses

Spicy Hot Cross Buns

3 cups ALL-PURPOSE FLOUR

2½ cups WHOLEWHEAT FLOUR

1½ tsp. SALT

1½ tsp. GROUND ALLSPICE

1 tsp. GROUND CINNAMON

½ tsp. GROUND NUTMEG

4 tbsp. BUTTER

grated rind 1 LEMON

⅓ cup SOFT LIGHT BROWN SUGAR

1 package QUICK-RISE YEAST

⅓ cup MIXED PEEL

½ cup CURRANTS

⅓ cup RAISINS

1 EGG, BEATEN

½ cup PLAIN YOGURT

1 cup LUKEWARM WATER

For the crosses

¾ cup ALL-PURPOSE FLOUR

½ tsp. SALT

6 tbsp. COLD WATER

Glaze

1 EGG, BEATEN

Icing

2 tbsp. COLD WATER

¼ cup GRANULATED SUGAR

Grease a 13 × 9 × 2-inch baking pan. Sift the flour, salt and spices into a bowl. Rub in the butter, then stir in the lemon rind, sugar, yeast, peel, and dried fruit. Beat the egg, yogurt and lukewarm water together, then add to the bowl and mix to a soft dough. Turn the dough onto a lightly floured surface and knead well for 8 to 10 minutes until smooth and elastic. Divide into 15 even pieces. Roll each piece into a round ball, then place in 3 rows of 5, in the pan. Completely cover with oiled plastic wrap and leave until doubled in size for about 1½ hours.

Preheat the oven to 425°F. Mix together the ingredients for the crosses and spoon into a pastry bag fitted with a ¼-inch plain round tip. Brush the buns with beaten egg, then pipe a whole line of paste from one end to the other. Repeat the other way until all the buns are crossed. Bake for 25 to 30 minutes, reducing the temperature to 350°F after 10 minutes. Dissolve the sugar and water together to make the finishing glaze. Turn out the buns and brush with the glaze while still hot.

MAKES 15

RIGHT: Spicy Hot Cross Buns

Greek Easter Egg Breads

1 quantity ENRICHED DOUGH, (SEE PAGE 32)
8 EGGS, AT ROOM TEMPERATURE
BEATEN EGG TO GLAZE

Divide the dough into 8 pieces and place in an oiled plastic bag. Cut 1 piece into 3 and roll into 10-inch sausages and braid together. Stand the braid on its side, make into an oval and join the edges. Repeat with the remaining dough and place on a greased baking sheet. Put an egg into each nest, brush the dough with beaten egg, cover with oiled plastic wrap and leave to rise until doubled in size.

Preheat the oven to 400°F. Bake for 20 minutes until golden. Allow to cool. Serve warm, or paint with non-toxic pens and serve cold. Eat the egg with the bread.

MAKES 8

Kulich

1 cup MILK
4 strands SAFFRON
2 cakes FRESH YEAST
or
2 packages DRY YEAST
7¾ cups ALL-PURPOSE FLOUR
6 tbsp. HONEY
2 sticks (1 cup) BUTTER
4 EGG YOLKS
1 tsp. VANILLA
½ tsp. SALT
grated rind ½ LEMON
3 CARDAMOM SEEDS, CRUSHED
⅓ cup RAISINS
⅓ cup CANDIED PEELS, CHOPPED
½ cup RAISINS
⅓ cup SLIVERED ALMONDS
BEATEN EGG TO GLAZE

Glacé icing
1 cup CONFECTIONER'S SUGAR MIXED WITH
1 tsp. each WATER AND LEMON JUICE
COLORED SUGAR TO DECORATE

Heat the milk and saffron strands together to just below boiling. Leave to infuse until lukewarm. Reactivate the yeast with 4 tbsp. lukewarm water and leave until frothy. Whisk one third of the flour into the cooled milk, with 1 tbsp. of the honey and the yeast liquid. Whisk well and leave to stand for 1 hour.

Melt the butter with the remaining honey, cool and beat in the egg yolks. Whisk into the flour batter with the vanilla extract. Sift in the remaining flour and salt, knead together for 5 minutes until smooth, then knead in the remaining ingredients. Knead well until elastic, then replace in the bowl, cover with oiled plastic wrap and leave until doubled in size. Grease and line 3 × 1 lb.13 oz empty fruit cans or 2 × 3 lb shortening cans with buttered foil, so that the foil extends 2 inches beyond the top rim of the can. Knead the dough to knock out the air, shape into cylindrical rolls and place in the cans, half full. Prove until doubled in size. Brush with the egg glaze. Preheat the oven to 425°F. Bake for 5 minutes, then reduce heat to 400°F and bake 25 to 30 minutes longer. Remove from the cans to cool, then decorate with glacé icing and colored sugar.

MAKES 2 LARGE OR 3 SMALL CAKES

LEFT: Greek Easter Egg Breads
RIGHT: Kulich

Grittibanz

Grittibanz is traditionally eaten in Switzerland on December 6, to celebrate St Nicholas's Day.

1 *quantity* ENRICHED DOUGH (SEE PAGE 32)

3 RAISINS

1 EGG, BEATEN

Divide the dough into thirds. Roll out two thirds into a 9-inch square. Using a tea cup and plate as a guide, cut out rounds for body and head. Place on a greased baking sheet ½ inch apart. Make the arms, take scraps and roll into a strand 7 inches long. Arrange round the top of the body. For hat and beard, use half the remaining third of dough. Roll into a 4-inch square and cut in half diagonally. Place 1 triangle on the head for the hat, shaping, and finish with a pom-pom. Place the other triangle at the base of the head for beard, pulling up the edges around the face for whiskers. Use the remaining dough to make eyes, brows, nose, moustache, hands and feet. Twist strands across the body for the belt. Push in the raisins for buttons. Brush with the beaten egg and leave to rise until doubled in size. Preheat the oven to 400°F. Bake for 20 to 25 minutes until crisp.   MAKES 1

Hungarian Poppy Seed Bread

4 *cups* ALL-PURPOSE FLOUR

½ *tsp.* SALT

1 *package* QUICK-RISE YEAST

⅓ *cup* GRANULATED SUGAR

2 *tsp.* GRATED LEMON RIND

1 EGG, BEATEN

1 *cup* LUKEWARM MILK

⅓ *cup* UNSALTED BUTTER, MELTED, COOLED

Filling

½ *cup* POPPY SEEDS

2 *tbsp.* BUTTER

2 *tbsp.* HONEY

1 *cup* WALNUT PIECES, CHOPPED

1 *tbsp.* FINELY GRATED LEMON RIND

1 *tsp.* CINNAMON

1 EGG WHITE, BEATEN UNTIL STIFF

Glaze

1 EGG, BEATEN WITH 2 TBSP. WATER

Sift the flour and salt together and stir in the yeast, sugar and lemon rind. Beat together the egg, lukewarm milk and melted butter and add to the dry ingredients. Mix to a soft dough and knead well for 8 minutes until soft, smooth and elastic. Replace in the bowl, cover with oiled plastic wrap and leave to rise until doubled, for 1 hour.

Make the filling: mix poppy seeds with the butter and remaining ingredients. Roll out the dough to 2 rectangles 18 × 12 inches. Spread the filling over the 2 pieces of dough, then roll each piece up, jelly-roll fashion.

Coil each roll round, then place on greased baking sheets and brush with egg glaze. Leave to prove until doubled in size. Preheat the oven to 350°F and bake for 35 minutes.   MAKES 2

LEFT: Grittibanz

RIGHT: Hungarian Poppy Seed Bread

Cholla

Cholla is the traditional Jewish Friday night Sabbath bread, being easy to break without using a knife. A round, coiled Cholla or Challah is made for Jewish New Year to represent peace, unity and the year to come.

1 cup BOILING WATER

FEW SAFFRON STRANDS

1 cake FRESH YEAST

1 tsp. HONEY

4 cups UNBLEACHED ALL-PURPOSE FLOUR

1 tsp. SALT

2 tbsp. VEGETABLE OIL

1 EGG, BEATEN

Glaze

1 EGG, BEATEN WITH

2 tbsp. WATER

POPPY SEEDS TO DECORATE

Pour the boiling water over the saffron strands, then leave to infuse until lukewarm. Strain out the saffron.

Crumble the yeast into 3 tbsp. of the water and stir in the honey. Leave to froth for 5 minutes. Sift the flour and salt into a bowl, add the yeast liquid, water, oil, and beaten egg. Mix to a soft dough, then turn out and knead until smooth and elastic, for about 8 minutes.

Return to the bowl and cover with oiled plastic wrap. Leave to rise until doubled in size. Knock back the dough to punch out all the air, then divide into 2 pieces, one twice the size of the other. Roll the larger piece into 3 strands 12 inches long and braid them. Roll the smaller piece into 3 strands 8 inches long and braid them. Place the small braid on top of the larger one. Pinch the ends together and place the loaf on an oiled baking sheet. Leave to double in size.

Preheat the oven to 400°F. Brush with beaten egg, then sprinkle with poppy seeds. Bake for 10 minutes, reduce to 375°F and bake for 35 to 40 minutes longer.

MAKES 1

Bulkalech (Wedding rolls) Weigh one batch of Cholla dough (see above) into 2 oz pieces. Divide each piece into 2, weighing ½ oz and 1½ oz each.

Roll each piece into a thin sausage. Place the small strip diagonally on top of the larger one to make a cross. Twist the long ends over the short piece, then loop short ends round to make a knot.

Tuck ends underneath, place on an oiled baking sheet and leave to double in size, covered in oiled plastic wrap.

Preheat the oven to 400°F. Brush with egg glaze and bake for 10 minutes until lightly browned.   MAKES 12

TOP: *Bulkalech*

BOTTOM: *Cholla*

Breads with Fillings

Add a savory filling to a basic bread dough and you have an instant meal. You'll find these international favorites are easy to make and great for parties or supper dishes.

Pizza

1 package DRY YEAST
1 tsp. GRANULATED SUGAR
1 cup LUKEWARM WATER
3½ cups ALL-PURPOSE FLOUR
½ tsp. SALT
2 tbsp. OLIVE OIL
4 tbsp. TOMATO PIZZA SAUCE
TOPPINGS OF CHOICE

Four Seasons
2 LARGE TOMATOES, SLICED
2 oz HAM OR SALAMI
1 cup BUTTON MUSHROOMS
1 × 2 oz CAN ANCHOVIES, DRAINED
1 × 14 oz CAN ARTICHOKE HEARTS, DRAINED, SLICED
⅓ cup BLACK OLIVES, PITTED AND SLICED
½ cup MOZZARELLA CHEESE, GRATED

Bacon and Cheese
4 SLICES BACON, FINELY CHOPPED
1 cup CHEDDAR CHEESE, GRATED
FRESH BASIL LEAVES, CHOPPED

Pepperoni
1 MEDIUM GREEN PEPPER, DESEEDED AND SLICED INTO RINGS
2 cups MUSHROOMS, SLICED
1 tbsp. OLIVE OIL
2 oz PEPPERONI SAUSAGE, SLICED
1 cup MOZZARELLA OR CHEDDAR CHEESE, GRATED

Sprinkle the dry yeast and sugar into the water and leave to stand for 20 minutes, until the liquid is frothy.

Sift the flour and salt into a bowl and add the yeast liquid with the oil. Mix to a soft dough and knead for 5 minutes until elastic and smooth. Cover with oiled plastic wrap and leave to rise until doubled in size, about 1 hour.

Punch the dough to knock out the air, then roll out to two 10 to 12-inch rounds and place on oiled baking sheets. Spread with tomato sauce and the topping of your choice. Leave to rise for 15 minutes until puffy. Meanwhile preheat the oven to 425°F. Bake for 20 to 25 minutes until crisp. MAKES 2

For four seasons sprinkle with the toppings and cheese and bake as above for 25 to 30 minutes.
For bacon and cheese sprinkle with toppings and bake as above.
For pepperoni spread the toppings onto the tomato sauce, brush the vegetables with olive oil, sprinkle with the cheese and bake as above.

RIGHT: Four Seasons Pizza

Lahma Bi Ajeen

This is an Arabic version of the traditional pizza. Eat these delicious mouthfuls rolled up.

1 *quantity* PIZZA DOUGH (SEE PAGE 84) MADE WITH
2 *cups* ALL-PURPOSE FLOUR AND
1½ *cups* WHOLEWHEAT FLOUR

Filling

2 *cups* ONIONS, CHOPPED
2 *tbsp.* OLIVE OIL
1 *lb* GROUND LAMB
1 × 14 *oz* CAN TOMATOES
4 *tbsp.* TOMATO PURÉE
½ *tsp.* GROUND ALLSPICE
PINCH EACH OF CAYENNE PEPPER
SALT AND BLACK PEPPER

Garnish

4 *tbsp.* CHOPPED FRESH PARSLEY AND
CORIANDER
2 *tbsp.* PINE NUTS, LIGHTLY TOASTED

Make up the pizza dough as on page 84, and leave to double in size, covered. Meanwhile, make the filling. Sauté the onions in the oil, add the lamb and cook until lightly browned. Add the tomatoes, tomato purée, allspice, cayenne, salt and pepper. Simmer until thick and pulpy, then cool. Knead the dough, punching back to knead out the air. Roll out the dough to ten 6-inch circles. Spread the cooled filling over the rounds to within ½ inch of edge. Place on oiled baking sheets and leave for 10 minutes to puff up. Preheat the oven to 425°F. Bake for 10 minutes, then serve immediately, sprinkled with herbs and toasted pine nuts. MAKES 10

Breaded Sausage Rolls

12 *oz* TRADITIONAL WHITE BREAD DOUGH
(SEE PAGE 14)
1 *lb* PORK SAUSAGEMEAT
2 *tsp.* MUSTARD
1 *cup* FINELY GRATED PARMESAN CHEESE

Make up the dough, leave to prove then knock back. Roll the risen dough to a rectangle 20 × 9 inches. Cut the dough in half lengthwise. Roll the sausagemeat into 20-inch lengths. Spread the dough with mustard, sprinkle with half the grated cheese and place one length of sausagemeat on each piece of dough. Roll up the dough round the sausagemeat and roll out to 18 inches using the palms of both hands. Cut into 16. Make slashes in the rolls, and sprinkle with remaining cheese.

Place on greased baking sheets and leave to rise for 30 minutes. Preheat the oven to 425°F. Bake for about 25 minutes. MAKES 32

LEFT: Lahma Bi Ajeen
RIGHT: Breaded Sausage Rolls

Baked Calzone

Calzone are basically pizzas, folded in half to enclose the filling, and traditionally deep fried in oil. Here is a more healthy version of this famous Italian hot sandwich.

1 quantity PIZZA DOUGH (SEE PAGE 84)

Glaze
3 tbsp. OLIVE OIL

Filling 1:
½ cup SOFT CREAM CHEESE WITH GARLIC AND HERBS
3 oz PARMA HAM OR SMOKED HAM, CHOPPED
1 × 14 oz can ARTICHOKE HEARTS, DRAINED, SLICED
1 cup MOZZARELLA CHEESE, GRATED

Filling 2:
1 tbsp. OLIVE OIL
1 CLOVE GARLIC, CRUSHED
1 lb RIPE TOMATOES, PEELED, SEEDED AND SLICED
¼ cup SUN-DRIED TOMATOES IN OIL, DRAINED, CHOPPED
1 tbsp. FRESH BASIL OR OREGANO
or
1 tsp. DRIED OREGANO
1 cup MOZZARELLA CHEESE, GRATED

Filling 3:
7 oz CANNED CANELLINI BEANS, DRAINED
¼ cup ITALIAN SALAMI, CHOPPED
1 BEEFSTEAK TOMATO, PEELED, SEEDED, CHOPPED
1 tbsp. FRESH SAGE, CHOPPED
¼ cup MOZZARELLA CHEESE, GRATED

Make up the pizza dough and leave until doubled in size. Knead to knock out the air. Divide the dough into 6 and roll out to 6-inch circles. Choose one of the fillings and make up separately. (Each batch of filling will fill one batch of dough.) Mix all the filling ingredients together and season with black pepper and a little salt.

Dampen the outside edges of the circles and divide the filling between them, placing the filling over one side of the dough in a half moon shape. Press the plain dough over and pinch the edges to seal.

Place on an oiled baking sheet and brush liberally all over with olive oil. Leave for 10 minutes until starting to puff up. Meanwhile, preheat the oven to 425°F. Bake for 15 minutes or until the bread dough sounds hollow when tapped.

For the traditional version, deep fry in vegetable oil for about 3 minutes until golden brown.   MAKES 6

RIGHT: Baked Calzone

Breads without Yeast

Rising agents such as soda will make breads rise quickly. These fast bakes don't involve the slower processes involved with yeast, but taste just as good.

Molasses Bread

3⅓ *cups* WHOLEWHEAT FLOUR

2 *cups* UNBLEACHED ALL-PURPOSE FLOUR

1 *tsp.* SALT

1 *tsp.* BAKING SODA

½ *tsp.* GROUND GINGER

2 *tbsp.* BUTTER

1 *cup* BUTTERMILK

2 *tbsp.* DARK MOLASSES

2 *tbsp.* GRANULATED SUGAR

1 EGG, BEATEN

Preheat the oven to 375°F. Grease two 8½ × 4¼ × 2¾-inch loaf pans, or two 8-inch round pans.

Sift the flours, salt, soda and ginger into a bowl and rub in the butter until it resembles fine crumbs. Beat the buttermilk, molasses, sugar and egg together and quickly stir into the dry ingredients. Mix to a rough dough then quickly place in the pans and bake for about 40 minutes until a toothpick inserted in the center comes out clean. Leave to cool but do not eat for 4 to 5 hours. This allows the bread to 'set'. MAKES 2 × 1 LB LOAVES

Potato Scones

1 *lb (2 large)* POTATOES

4 *tbsp.* BUTTER, SOFTENED

1 *cup* ALL-PURPOSE FLOUR

Peel the potatoes, boil until soft, then drain well and cool. Heat a griddle or heavy-based skillet. Unless using a non-stick skillet, rub with salt and paper towels, remove the salt then rub with wax paper and lard. Keep the griddle or skillet warm over a low heat.

Press the potatoes through a sieve, season well with salt, then beat in the butter and gradually work in the flour. Roll out to ¼ inch thick and cut into 2½-inch rounds or cut into squares. Place on the preheated griddle or skillet and cook for 2 to 3 minutes on each side until golden. Serve immediately, or cool on a wire rack and serve later after heating under the grill. MAKES 12

LEFT: Molasses Bread

RIGHT: Potato Scones

Prune Bread

1⅔ cups PITTED PRUNES, COARSELY CHOPPED

1 cup HOT TEA

½ cup SOFT DARK BROWN SUGAR

1 stick (½ cup) BUTTER

1¾ cups WHOLEWHEAT FLOUR

2½ tsp. BAKING POWDER

½ tsp. SALT

1 tsp. BAKING SODA

1 tsp. GROUND CINNAMON

½ cup MIXED CHOPPED NUTS

1 EGG, BEATEN

Place the prunes, hot tea, sugar and butter in a pan and heat to melt the sugar and butter. Leave to cool completely. Preheat the oven to 350°F. Grease a 9 × 5 × 3-inch loaf pan.

Sift the flour, baking powder, salt, soda and spice together, then beat in the cooled mixture with the nuts and egg. Spoon evenly into the pan, smooth the top and bake for 1 hour or until firm in the center. Cool in the pan, then keep for a day, wrapped tightly in foil. Serve sliced and buttered.

MAKES 1 × 2 LB LOAF

Banana Tea Bread

2 cups SELF-RISING FLOUR

¼ tsp. BAKING SODA

¼ tsp. SALT

6 tbsp. BUTTER

¾ cup LIGHT BROWN SUGAR

2 EGGS, BEATEN

1 lb (2 large) RIPE BANANAS, MASHED

1 cup WALNUT PIECES, CHOPPED

Preheat the oven to 350°F. Grease and line bottom of a 9 × 5 × 3-inch loaf pan.

Sift the flour, baking soda and salt together. Cream the butter and sugar until light and fluffy then beat in the eggs, adding a little of the flour with each addition. Fold in the remaining ingredients until smooth. Put in pan and bake for 1 hour or until golden and firm in the center.

MAKES 1 × 2 LB LOAF

Top: Prune Bread

Bottom: Banana Tea Bread

Breateakfast Muffins

Muffins are always popular for breakfast or brunch and they can be made in a matter of minutes.

2 cups ALL-PURPOSE FLOUR
1 tbsp. BAKING POWDER
½ tsp. BAKING SODA
2 tbsp. GRANULATED SUGAR
3 tbsp. SOFT LIGHT BROWN SUGAR
1 EGG
1 cup MILK
PINCH OF SALT
¼ cup BUTTER, MELTED

Cinnamon Muffins
½ cup ROLLED OATS
2 tsp. GROUND CINNAMON
2 tbsp. CLEAR HONEY
1 tbsp. ORANGE JUICE
1 cup RAISINS

Blueberry Muffins
½ cup GRANULATED SUGAR
½ cup FROZEN BLUEBERRIES OR
BLACKCURRANTS
FEW DROPS VANILLA

Choc Chip Muffins
4 tbsp. COCOA POWDER
⅔ cup SEMI-SWEET CHOCOLATE CHIPS
⅔ cup WHITE CHOCOLATE CHIPS

Banana Bran Muffins
1 cup NATURAL BRAN
2 large BANANAS, MASHED

Preheat the oven to 400°F. Place 10 large deep paper muffin liners in deep muffin pans. Sift the flour, baking powder, soda and sugars into a bowl and make a well in the center. Beat the egg, milk and salt together and add to the bowl with the melted butter. Lightly beat the mixture until well combined, but do not overbeat. Fold in any additional ingredients.

Fill the muffin liners three quarters full, then bake for 20 minutes until a toothpick inserted into the center comes out clean. Serve warm or cold.   MAKES 10 TO 12

For cinnamon muffins stir the oats and cinnamon into the dry ingredients. Add the honey and orange juice with the milk. Fold the raisins into the final mixture, then bake as above.

For blueberry muffins omit the brown sugar and use the amount of granulated sugar given here. Half thaw the blueberries or blackcurrants until starting to soften. Gently fold into the final mixture with the vanilla, and bake as above.

For choc chip muffins sift in the cocoa with the dry ingredients. Fold the chocolate chips into the final mixture, and bake as above.

For banana bran muffins stir the bran into the dry ingredients, add the bananas to the final mixture, and bake as above.

RIGHT: Breakfast Muffins

Index

Aberdeen rowies, buttery 56
All-purpose flour 8
American breads 62-6
Anadama bread 66
Apricot and honey loaf 28

Babas 52
Bacon and cheese pizza 84
Bagels 48
Baguettes 16
Baking 13
Banana bran muffins 94
  banana tea bread 92
Bara brith 56
Barm brack, Irish 34
Bath buns 34
Batter 12
Bishop's bread 74
Blinis 70
Bloomer 16
Blueberry muffins 94
Bread flour 8
Breaded sausage rolls 86
Breakfast muffins 94
Brioches, quick breakfast 36
British breads 54-60
Brown flour 8
Buckwheat flour 9
  blinis 70
Buns: Bath buns 34
  Chelsea buns 32
  spicy hot cross buns 76
Buttery Aberdeen rowies 56

Californian raisin bread 24
Calzone, baked 88
Chapatis 68
Cheese, sage and onion braid 18
Chelsea buns 32
Chocolate: choc chip muffins 94
  pains au chocolat 50
  Swedish twists and whirls 40
Cholla 82
Ciabatta 46
Cinnamon muffins 94
Cocks combs 42
Continental breads 42-52
Cornish saffron bread 60

Cornmeal 9
  Anadama bread 66
  corn husks 62
  cornmeal muffins 62
  Johnny cake 62
Cottage loaf 16
Country breads 18-28
Croissants 50
Crumpets 58

Danish pastries 42
  Swedish twists and whirls 40
Doughnuts 30
Dry yeast 10

Easter egg breads, Greek 78
Eastern breads 68-70
Enriched breads 30-40
Equipment 11

Fats 10
Festive breads 72-82
Finishes 16
Flat breads 68-70
Flours 8-9
Focaccia 44
Fougasses 74
Four seasons pizza 84
Freezing bread 10
French baguettes 16
Fresh yeast 10

Glazes 16
Gluten 12
Granary flour 8-9
Grant loaf 24
Greek Easter egg breads 78
Grissini 44
Grittibanz 80

Hedgehog rolls 16
Hot cross buns, spicy 76
Hungarian poppy seed bread 80

Ingredients 8-10
Irish barm brack 34

Johnny cake 62

Kneading 12
Knocking back 13
Kough-aman 38
Kugelhopf 50
Kulich 78

Lahma bi ajeen 86
Lardy cake 54
Liquids 10

Mixed grain flour 8-9
Mixed seed bread 26
Mixing 12
Molasses bread 90
Morning rolls 16
Muffins: breakfast muffins 94
  cornmeal muffins 62
  English muffins 58

Oats 9
  oat and honey loaf 20
Olive oil bread with sun-dried
  tomatoes 44

Pain de campagne 26
Pains au chocolat 50
Pane d'oro 40
Parathas 68
Parker House rolls 66
Pepperoni pizza 84
Pitas 70
Pizza 84
Plastic wrap 11
Potato scones 90
Pretzels 48
Proving dough 13
Prune bread 92
Pugilese 46

Quick-blend yeast 10

Rising dough 13
Rolls: hedgehog rolls 16
  morning rolls 16
  Parker House rolls 66
Rye flour 9
  rye bread 20
  rye sourdough 22

St. Lucia breads 72
Sally Lunn 38
Salt 9
Sausage rolls, breaded 86
Savarin 52
Scones, potato 90
Soda bread 60
Sourdough bread 22
  rye sourdough 22
Spicy hot cross buns 76
Sponge batter 12
Sticky fruit couronne 32
Stollen 72
Stoneground flours 9
Storing bread 10
Storing flour 9
Streusel-topped coffee bread 36
Swedish twists and whirls 40

Tea bread, banana 92
Techniques 12-13
Temperature, liquids 10
Testing 13
Toppings 16
Tortillas 64
Traditional white bread 14-15

Unbleached flours 9

Vienna bread 16

Wheat flour 8
Wheatmeal flour 8
White bread, traditional 14-15
White flour 8
Wholewheat bread, quick 18
Wholewheat flour 8
Windmills 42

Yeast 9-10
  making a yeast liquid 12
Yeastless breads 90-94

Zucchini bread 64